The Organic Manual

The
Organic Manual

Natural Gardening for the 21st Century

by

Howard Garrett

Tapestry Press
Arlington, Texas

Tapestry Press
3649 Conflans Road
Suite 103
Irving, TX 75061

Printed in the United States of America

05 04 03 02 01 5 4 3 2 1

Library of Congress Cataloging-in-Publication Data
Garrett, Howard, 1947-
    The organic manual : natural gardening for the 21st century /
by Howard Garrett.
        p. cm.
    ISBN 1-930819-16-1 (trade paper : alk. paper)
    1. Organic gardening. 2. Garden pests—Biological control. 3.
Plants, Protection of. I. Title.
    SB453.5 .G42 2001
    635'.0484—dc21
                                            2001008062

Book design and layout by
D. & F. Scott Publishing, Inc.
North Richland Hills, Texas

Some images copyright by www.arttoday.com
Cover design by Cheryl Corbitt and Rishi Seth

FOR LOGAN

Contents

Contents

FOREWORD

odern communications and the increased speed of travel have virtually turned the whole planet into our visible landscape. There are no new frontiers. Most habitable land is being used and abused with the overuse of chemical fertilizers and toxic pesticides.

Thinking people are quickly realizing the pollution this adds to our already overburdened environment. But although information on natural organic farming and vegetable gardening is becoming more and more available, the commercial landscape contractor and the urban dweller with the small bit of Nature surrounding his home has up until now been mostly forgotten.

Now, with the *Organic Manual*, Howard Garrett has met this need. The *Organic Manual* combines Howard's immense knowledge of and experience in landscape design and installation with his desire to work in harmony with Nature. It's a masterpiece for the home and commercial landscaper.

Howard has a great talent for communicating and the courage it takes to tell the truth. His book not only points out the damage some horticultural chemicals do and shows how they lead down a dead-end road, but gives sensible, earth-friendly alternatives that perform as well as and, in the long run, better than toxic chemicals.

Whenever someone speaks out to try to change the current system, he is sure to draw criticism, and I imagine that Howard Garrett has and will draw his share. But, then, how long can the truth be criticized?

Malcolm Beck

Organic Farmer
Founder of Garden-Ville
Author of *The Garden-Ville Method: Lessons in Nature, Secret Life of Compost, Texas Organic Vegetable Gardening,* and *Texas Bug Book.*

ACKNOWLEDGMENTS

I would like to thank all of the people in the world who have devoted years of their lives to advancing the practice of organics. Among them are Sir Albert Howard, William Albrecht, J. I. and Robert Rodale, Charles Walters, Dr. Phil Callahan, Bargyla Rateaver, Arden Anderson, and Malcolm Beck.

Thanks also go to the people who taught me the most about organics and least-toxic pest controls. They include Dr. Dan Clair with the Texas Department of Agriculture, Dr. Paul Syltie, Dr. Robert Petit, T. L. Senn, Elliott C. Roberts, John Dromgoole, and Malcolm Beck.

I would also like to thank those people who have helped me in their own ways: Judy Garrett, Stan Wetsel, Walter Dahlberg, Barbara Sargent, Carol Harrison, Alan Shipley, Sam Frenkil, Bill Neiman, Kim Sinks, Rob Nalley, Derek Little, Jim Marshall, Bobby Spence, Charlie Sikes, Jo Harrell, Patti Lancaster, Kevin Starnes, Tracy Fields, Odena Brannam, Louise Riotte, Walt Davis, Wes Culwell, Joe, Peggy, and Dalton Maddox, Alan Savory, Dick and Pat Richardson, Cary Hardin, Ruth and Dick Kinler, Greg Rohde, Ronnie Felderhoff, Greg Teets, Mark Rose, Tom Anderson, Judy Griffin, Malcolm Bayless, Barbara Pletcher, Bob Scott, Frank Sheffler, Lee Steele, Tim Bolinger, Alex Burton, Barney Lipscomb, Carlton Turner, Marie Calliet, Sabino Cortez, Tex Gross, Mary Herrick, Phil Huey, Jim Jones, Clint Josey, Rosa Finsley, George Diggs, Bob O'Kennon, Dick Lentz, Paul Tomaso, Tom Ohrstrum, Mike Casey, Jimmy Joe Wiley, Jon Pinkus, Gary Olp, Jeff Resnick, Joe Robertson, Ralph Ryan, Allan Nation, Bobby Smith, Rick Sowders, Barbara and Paul Stitt, Sally Fallon, Joe McFarland, Charlie Townsend, K. Chandler, Shannon Davies, Tom Chapman, Ron Greenwood, Craig Verwers, Kari Rollins, Dottie Woodson, Betty Clark, Carl Whitcomb, William Rhea, Jo Robinson, and, of course, my readers and listeners, and Jewell and Ruby Garrett.

Thanks should also go to my clients who have been open-minded enough to allow organic techniques and products to be used on their properties. They include Interstate Realty in Memphis, Tennessee;

Acknowledgments

Alcon Laboratories in Fort Worth, Texas; Frito-Lay National Headquarters in Plano, Texas; Johnson & Johnson Medical; Collin County Community College District; Carrington Laboratories; Sabre Corporation; and many farmers, ranchers, and residential friends.

ABOUT THE AUTHOR

Howard Garrett is a 1969 graduate of Texas Tech University. He is a landscape architect, publisher, columnist, broadcaster, and organic horticulturist from Pittsburg, Texas. He currently lives in Dallas with his wife Judy and daughter Logan.

In 1988 Howard committed his entire career to the research into, education about, and promotion of organic landscaping, gardening, farming, and basic soil management. He has converted several commercial projects to organic programs. Among them are the corporate facilities of Frito-Lay in Plano, Johnson and Johnson in Arlington, and Sabre Corporation in Southlake, Texas. The 100-acre campus of Collin County Community College was the first of these large-scale commercial successes.

Thousands of homeowners have now switched to his organic program. Not only are these properties doing well, but they are in better shape than they ever were on synthetic chemical programs. The public has responded so positively to organics that there are more than 60 totally organic retail centers in north Texas and more than 500 that sell all the organic products.

Howard is host of the WBAP gardening show *The Natural Way* on Saturdays and Sundays and columnist for *The Dallas Morning News* "The Natural Way" in Friday's House and Garden section.

Howard has written many books, including: *Plants of the Metroplex, Howard Garrett's Texas Organic Gardening, Landscape Design . . . Texas Style, The Organic Manual, The Dirt Doctor's Guide to Organic Gardening, Plants for Texas, Texas Organic Vegetable Gardening, Texas Bug Book,* and *Herbs for Texas*. The vegetable gardening and bug books were coauthored with Malcolm Beck.

INTRODUCTION

rganics is the thoughtful and sensitive use of techniques and products that not only sustain but improve soil health and the environment in general.

Organic programs are really quite simple. Their success requires understanding that Nature cannot be divided into parts. Nothing can be added or taken away without causing a chain reaction. Creation, birth, death, decay, and rebirth are all elements in the chain of life and are all connected.

The practice of growing plants using organic techniques has been used for as long as man has walked the earth. Only since World War II has the world of agriculture and horticulture been changed by the introduction of toxic synthetic fertilizers and pesticides. The proliferation of these man-made chemicals temporarily increased the yield of many food crops and ornamentals, but it also increased the long-term cost of production, caused pollution of our air and drinking water, changed the soil structure, accelerated erosion, and jarred the entire ecosystem. The earth's fertile land has been depleted, and overall quality of production has decreased due to a dramatic reduction of the soil's health.

Reasons for the continued use of synthetic products include a lack of understanding of how organic techniques work and the fear that, if chemicals are discontinued, plants won't grow well and will be devoured by insects and disease. The amount of money spent on synthetic chemical advertising and research at major universities is of no small consequence either. Many people simply don't know that organic products work effectively and economically and are easy and fun to use. On the other hand, most folks don't realize how dangerous and damaging harsh pesticides and synthetic fertilizers are, not only to themselves, but to the health of the planet.

CHEMICALS VS. ORGANICS

It's not a chemical vs. organics question. Everything in the world is chemical. Even air and water are composed of chemicals such as hydrogen, oxygen, nitrogen, and carbon.

The words "chemical" and "organic" are equally misused and misunderstood. For example, there are products acceptable for use in an organic program that have low toxicity but are not truly organic, and some organic products are extremely dangerous and not acceptable in a wise organic program.

The point is that the two words, "chemical" and "organic," have become the passwords for the two philosophies. "Chemical" represents the university-taught approach of force-feeding the plants using synthetic fertilizers and trying to control Nature using synthetic pesticides, while "organic" represents the approach of working with Nature to improve soil health and using only products that increase the chemical, physical, and biological balance in the soil.

It's a big misconception that organic methods are simply safer ways to kill pests. The basis of organics is an overall philosophy of life more than a simple decision about which kinds of garden or farming products to use. The organic philosophy relates to the ability to see and understand Nature's systems and work within those systems. The chemical philosophy teaches that man and his products can control Nature. But Nature can't be controlled—it's really futile even to try. Many farmers have come to see that, and they are now realizing that we must stop taking the carbon and the life out of the soil and the land out of production. The landscaping industry is also moving, although slowly, toward the organic philosophy, primarily because of the tremendous public demand for safer and more environmentally sensitive techniques and products.

Another difference in philosophy relates to fertilization. Traditional "chemical" proponents say that plants must be fertilized with a 3–1–2 or 4–1–2 ratio fertilizer four times a year. The organic philosophy contends that the soil should be fed and balanced and that plants don't need to be force-fed. Balancing the soil is not discussed very often, if ever, in the synthetic chemical programs.

The balance of chemistry, physics, and biology is the key. If the soil is biologically healthy, the physics and chemistry will also be in balance. The pH will be between 6.2 and 6.5, and earthworms and microbes will be in the proper populations. In healthy soil calcium will represent approximately 60–70 percent of the available chemical nutrients, magnesium 10–20 percent, potassium 2–5 percent, and sodium .5–3 percent, and all the trace elements should be in their proper relative proportions.

Another advantage of balanced soil chemistry is that fertilizer inputs can be greatly reduced. Once the soil is balanced properly, the maintenance of plants can be done primarily with mulches, organic matter, foliar feeding, and an occasional application of carbon-based fertilizers.

A chemically, physically, and biologically balanced soil will have proper tilth (state of aggregation or crumbliness), positive drainage, and the correct populations of living organisms. All you have to do is stop killing the life in the soil with the quick-fix poisons. The end result is healthy plants, animals and people.

REVERSING THE CHEMICAL ADDICTION

There are two major soil pollutants—unbalanced, high-nitrogen, synthetic fertilizers and toxic pesticides. Synthetic fertilizers are the most common chemicals used in farming, gardening, and landscaping. These man-made fertilizers are merely soluble-salt compounds, usually found in granulated form, and relatively inexpensive. Synthetic fertilizers provide nothing to benefit the soil; in fact, they leave considerable amounts of salt residue and other contamination. Their most serious flaw is the lack of carbon.

Since the plants will not absorb large quantities of salt, continued use of salt-based fertilizers can lead to loss of plant quality, loss of productivity, and, in extreme cases, phytotoxicity (poisoning of the plants). These fertilizers repel and kill beneficial soil microorganisms and earthworms, they are harsh and interfere with the natural chemical, physical, and biological systems in the soil, and they feed plants too fast with an incomplete diet.

High levels of nitrates, which are created by synthetic nitrogen fertilizers, are carcinogenic and frequently show up in our drinking water. Because of the overuse of high nitrogen fertilizers and the plant's inability to use large amounts of nitrogen, the excess is simply leached or washed away and ends up ultimately in our streams, lakes, and aquifers.

Pesticides are the second most common chemicals applied to plants and soil. Pesticides include insecticides, fungicides, herbicides, rodenticides, and any other poisons used to kill plants or animals. Excess pesticides destroy the microscopic living organisms of the soil. Pesticides will also affect plant growth, and, when absorbed by the plant, begin passing through the food chain. All living organisms are affected—microorganisms, insects, animals, and man. If used too often at excessive rates, pesticides can virtually sterilize the soil if leaching does not occur—and of course the leaching causes other problems.

When pesticides are leached out of the soil, they end up in streams or ground water, available to enter the food chain. Huge amounts of toxic chemicals are used on home lawns and agricultural crops, making the use of chemicals a serious problem in urban as well as rural areas. Insects and diseases get blamed for the use of these toxins, but they are not the problem, only the symptom of the problem. The real problem is poor soil health, and that problem is increased with each application of toxic chemicals. Chemical programs create a drug dependency and, unfortunately, they have controlled mainstream agriculture and horticulture.

The damage to our soil's health can be reversed by returning it to a natural balance. Those of us in the landscape industry and the agriculture industry must take the lead, but homeowners must also get involved in reducing and ultimately eliminating the toxic chemicals we dump into our environment. Besides being dangerous, they aren't necessary. The organic method works better.

Thirty-five years ago, J. I. and Robert Rodale began the organic movement in the United States using the studies and writings of Sir Albert Howard of England and Dr. William A. Albrecht of the University of Missouri. Rodale convinced many home gardeners and some farmers to add humus to the soil through organic matter and minerals through natural rock powders to improve the health and nutrition of food crops. The idea was quite simple: healthy soil produces healthy plants; healthy plants produce healthy animals and humans. It's possible that the simplicity has been one of the major roadblocks. How could something so simple work? A more powerful obstacle has been the concern, "How are we going to make money?"

The purpose of this book is to explain how the natural organic method works and what products are best to use in a complete organic program. The goal is to convince you to use the organic method on farm, ranch, landscaping, and greenhouse operations.

You will learn that organic land management offers reduced long-term costs and liabilities and creates and maintains a safe, healthy environment for all concerned.

Food crops grown organically are a critical ingredient in eliminating disease. The elimination of pesticide residue is important, but not the most important issue. Health is the primary issue, and real health comes from eating food containing a proper balance of mineral nutrients and energy. Healthy food can only come from healthy soil.

HEALTHY SOILS

oil and dirt are two very different things. Dirt is an inert planting medium that holds up plants. Soil is a wonderfully dynamic, ever-changing, complex, living system of life, energy, and minerals. Soil, like all parts of the environment, is fragile. It is also hard to repair once damaged. Unfortunately, most conventional landscape and agriculture procedures have damaged and are continuing to damage the soil. The key is to stop the damage by starting to use management techniques, soil amendments, fertilizers, and pest control products that benefit soil health.

Soil, along with water, air, and sunlight, is one of the basic building blocks of life on earth.

For years the soil has been abused. Man has for so long taken from the land without giving back that the soil in much of the world has died and become desert where it was once thriving and productive. Deserts aren't just sand dunes. Dead lakes and rivers are deserts. Chemically abused farms and chemically treated urban lawns are deserts. The definition of "desert" is land that has lost its biological diversity. We can reverse the trend by preserving healthy soil and rebuilding dead and unbalanced soil. We must reestablish biodiversity. A mix of microbes, insects, snakes, toads, lizards, birds, mammals, annuals, perennials, trees, grasses, herbs, and wildflowers all must be present. Large masses of one plant type or monocultures must be eliminated. Nature abhors straight lines, vacuums, and monocultures. Forests that have been replanted with only one tree species after clear cutting are "deserts." Desertification of the world must end or the world might end—earlier than scheduled!

Healthy soil is a balance of physics, chemistry, and biology. It is a mixture of minerals, organic matter, living organisms, water, and air. It contains 25 percent air, 25 percent water, 45 percent minerals, 5 percent humus, and active populations of living organisms. Healthy soil is aerated, rich in organic matter, and alive with insects, earthworms, and microscopic plants and animals. It is well drained, sweet smelling, moist, and rich in a wide variety of minerals and nutrients. It is also highly energized.

*Healthy soil is a dynamic living community
of air, water, organic matter, minerals,
and living organisms.*

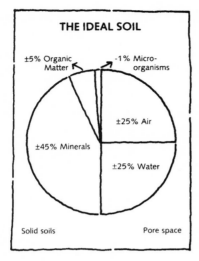

THE IDEAL SOIL

±5% Organic Matter

-1% Micro-organisms

±25% Air

±45% Minerals

±25% Water

Solid soils

Pore space

ORGANIC MATTER

Organic matter is anything that was once living. Every living thing dies, and everything that dies, rots. All organic matter biodegrades. It's during that process that microorganisms reduce once-living matter into basic elements of fertility.

It's the constant tilling of the soil, and removal of organic matter without replenishment that will ultimately reduce the soil to an inorganic state, rendering it useless for healthy plant growth.

When organic matter, such as leaves, breaks down, becoming dark brown and crumbly, the resulting product is humus. Humus is soft, crumbly, amorphous, and sweet smelling. It holds and slowly releases water, minerals, and nutrients to the plants.

Maintaining a constant supply of organic matter is essential to start and continue an organic program. Good sources of organic matter for the soil include composted materials, green cover crops, vegetable and animal waste, root exudates, and the dead bodies of insects and microorganisms.

SOIL MICROORGANISMS

You don't hear much about soil microorganisms from the chemically conventional horticulturists and farmers. Microorganisms are microscopic plants and animals. They are the "life" in the soil. They include bacteria, fungi, actinomycetes, algae, protozoa, yeast, germs, ground pearls, and nematodes. There are about 50 billion microbes in 1 tablespoon of soil.

There are approximately 900,000,000,000 (nine hundred billion) microorganisms per pound of healthy soil.

To give you a clear idea of the population of these vital microbes, the estimated numbers of common organisms found in each gram of reasonably healthy agricultural soils are as follows:

Bacteria	3,000,000	to	500,000,000
Actinomycetes	1,000,000	"	20,000,000
Fungi	5,000	"	1,000,000
Yeast	1,000	"	1,000,000
Protozoa	1,000	"	500,000
Algae	1,000	"	500,000
Nematodes	10	"	5,000

Note: 1 gram is the approximate weight of a paper clip.

The microorganisms' primary job is to break down organic matter—first into humus, then humic acid, and ultimately into basic elements. This process is known as mineralization. Microbes must have a constant supply of organic matter or they will be reduced in population and weaken the soil. Certain microorganisms also have the ability to fix nitrogen from the air, which is approximately 80 percent nitrogen. Unhealthy soil will not support plant growth without artificial foods and stimulants. Healthy soils produce food through microbial feeding. Microbes are constantly being born and are constantly dying. It's okay for microorganisms to die because that is the natural process. The dead bodies of microorganisms are actually an important source of organic matter in healthy soil.

Soil moisture is important to the health of microorganisms. Beneficial microbes thrive in soil that is neither dry nor soggy but about as wet as a squeezed-out sponge. Healthy soil is easier to keep at the proper moisture level and can help to save money on water bills. Biologically active organic soil can save as much as 50 percent of the water normally used for irrigation of soil where large quantities of harsh pesticides and synthetic fertilizers are used.

Most microorganisms need a constant supply of oxygen. Therefore, aeration of unhealthy soil is critical in the beginning for soil improvement.

ALGAE: Algae account for the majority of the photosynthetic microflora of the soil. They thrive primarily on or near the soil surface where light and moisture are adequate, although some algae can always be found in the subsoil. Algae produce organic matter by taking carbon dioxide from the air and energy from sunlight to create new cells. Fungi and bacteria can reduce the net amount of organic  matter, but algae increase the volume. They are much less numerous than bacteria, fungi, and actinomycetes but are extremely important. Blue-green algae (also called cyanobacteria) are able to fix or grab nitrogen directly from the air in the soil.

NEMATODES: Nematodes are probably the most numerous multicellular creatures on earth. They are active, tubular, microscopic animals living on moist surfaces or in liquid environments like the films of water in the soil. Destructive and beneficial nematodes exist in all soils. Some create knots on roots and some enter through lesions to feed on roots. Some species of beneficial nematodes are effective for the  control of termites, grubworms, fire ants, fleas, and other pests.

BACTERIA: Bacteria thrive under a wide variety of conditions from acid to alkaline and from aerobic (with free oxygen) to anaerobic (lack of free oxygen). Bacteria help in the decay of organic matter, encourage organic and inorganic chemical reactions that have a profound effect on plant growth, and fix nitrogen from the air in the soil. Most bacteria are found in the top one foot or so of soil.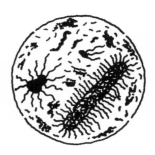

ACTINOMYCETES: Actinomycetes generally thrive in well-aerated, neutral to alkaline soils. They are less active in acid or waterlogged soils but are extremely important to the decay of organic matter in dry regions. They are visible as the white, fungus-like threads on decaying organic matter. The earthy smell of newly plowed soil or the forest floor is compliments of actinomycetes. They are a higher form of  bacteria and similar to fungi and molds. Actinomycetes are very important in the formulation of humus. Actinomycetes may work near the surface or many feet below the surface. While decomposing animal and vegetable matter, actinomycetes liberate carbon, nitrogen, and ammonia, making mineral nutrients available for higher plants.

PROTOZOA: Protozoa are the simplest form of animals. They are single-celled and microscopic in size. They obtain their food from organic matter. Protozoa serve to regulate the size of the bacterial community.

FUNGI: Fungi are multi-celled and filamentous or single-celled primitive plants. They lack chlorophyll and therefore lack the ability to make their own carbohydrates. Fungi thrive mainly in well-drained, neutral to acidic, oxygenated soils. Mycorrhizal fungi help the development of healthy root systems by growing on roots and effectively enlarging the length and surface area of roots. Some fungi are visible as  white, cobweb-like threads that actually enter the cells of the root hairs.

SOIL MACROORGANISMS

Healthy soil is not only full of billions of microorganisms, but it also contains many macroorganisms. These organisms can be seen with the naked eye. They range from tiny mites to large rodents and all have a specific function or purpose in the soil. The most famous and most helpful macroorganism is the earthworm. Earthworms till and aerate the soil, increase drainage, stimulate microbiotic activity, and increase soil fertility. It's impossible to have too many earthworms.

Macroorganisms can be divided into three major subgroups: herbivores, detritivores, and carnivores, although some may fit into more than one subgroup. Herbivores feed on living plants, detritivores feed on dead and decaying plant tissues, and carnivores feed on other living organisms (both micro and macroorganisms). Herbivores (plant eaters) include snails, slugs, insect larvae, termites, beetle larvae, woodchucks, mice, and grubs. Detritivores (decaying matter eaters) include mites, snails, beetles, millipedes, woodlice, springtails, earthworms, worms, spiders, scorpions, centipedes, earwigs, crickets, termites, slugs, and ants. Carnivores (animal eaters) include mites, springtails, enchytraeds, centipedes, snails, slugs, flies, moles, ants, spiders, centipedes, scorpions, and beetles.

Macroorganisms loosen the soil by burrowing and digging, help decompose plant tissue for use by microorganisms, and help to create beneficial compounds that plants can utilize. For example, earthworms, as they burrow up and down, will bring valuable minerals from deep in the soil up to the surface. These minerals can be used by the plant, and the burrowing helps oxygenate the root zone. Earthworms also take organic matter from the surface and pull it down into the soil to help build the carbon storehouse.

While some macroorganisms can be considered harmful or destructive to plant roots, their presence may also be valuable to the health of the soil. They may be an important food source for other organisms. The principles of organics teach that helping all pieces of Nature work in harmony is essential. If we try to kill all the macroorganisms that are detrimental, we will certainly kill the beneficial ones as well. Balance in a healthy soil is the goal. When the balance is disrupted, the symptoms of insects and diseases attack plant crops.

MINERALS

The soil's most plentiful major component is mineral matter. In the top 6" of healthy soil, the mineral portion will be approximately 45 percent. The mineral composition is the principal determinant of the soil's property. Minerals occur as a result of the physical or chemical action of the parent rock near the surface of the soil. There are more than 92 naturally-occurring mineral elements.

Minerals are responsible for the growth of a plant's cells. Plants depend on three essential nutrients derived from carbon dioxide and water: carbon, hydrogen, and oxygen. Plants also depend on thirteen essential nutrients derived from the minerals in the soil as inorganic salts—iron, potassium, calcium, magnesium, nitrogen, phosphorus, sulfur, manganese, chlorine, boron, zinc, copper, and molybdenum. The other 70 or so trace minerals are not fully understood but are important to the soil, to plants, and to Nature's whole.

Organic fertilizers do not have very high amounts of nitrogen, phosphorus, and potassium. When fertilizing or adding mineral nutrients, it's important to think about balance. Healthy soils and plants have a balance of elements and ingredients. A proper fertilization program will help keep that balance intact. That's why it's important to avoid an overkill of the well-known elements nitrogen, phosphorus, and potassium.

Here's a good example. The following are the percentages of various elements in whole plants:

Oxygen	45 percent
Carbon	44 percent
Hydrogen	6 percent
Nitrogen	2 percent
Potassium	1.1 percent
Phosphorus	0.4 percent
Sulfur	0.5 percent
Calcium	0.6 percent
Magnesium	0.3 percent

Note the relatively low percentages of nitrogen, phosphorus, and potassium and the high percentages of oxygen, carbon, and hydrogen.

When buying fertilizer, remember how relatively unimportant nitrogen, phosphorus, and potassium are. Think in terms of providing to the soil those products and elements that will help maintain the natural balance. If the soil is in a healthy, balanced condition (which includes organic matter and air), nitrogen, potassium, and phosphorus will be produced naturally by the feeding of microoganisms and relatively little will need to be added.

MINERAL NUTRIENTS

OXYGEN is an often overlooked element. Adding oxygen to most soils can cause an immediate response in plants, much the same effect as using high-nitrogen fertilizer. Oxygen can be added to the soil by mechanical means such as aerating, ripping, or tilling, but it also can be gotten indirectly by using organic fertilizers and soil conditioners. Healthy plants' extensive root systems can also can be very beneficial for introducing oxygen into the all-important top 12" of soil.

NITROGEN is an essential constituent of proteins and vital to plant health. However, excessive nitrogen can cause an imbalance in plant metabolism, which can adversely affect plant growth, fruiting, and storage life.

Nitrogen is an ingredient of proteins and distinguishes them from carbohydrates. The amount of nitrogen in a given material is determined by dividing the percent of protein by 6.25. Cottonseed meal, for example, is 60 percent protein. Dividing 60 by 6.25 equals 9.6 percent nitrogen. Unlike other nutrients, it does not originate from the soil but from the air. Nitrogen enters the soil through rain or by being fixed by living organisms associated with legumes such as clover, peas, beans, and alfalfa. Some organisms such as blue-green algae can fix nitrogen without an association with plants. The air is approximately 80 percent nitrogen. Lack of vigor and yellowing of the oldest leaves are signs of nitrogen deficiency.

PHOSPHATE is the soil's catalyst. Its most important function is to help transfer the energy in the plant from one point to another. Adequate phosphorus is needed for color and vitality of the plant at bloom time and at maturity. It also increases seed and flower size. Soils must have high levels of phosphates so that enough sugars are formed in the plants. Sources include: colloidal phosphate, superphosphate, rock phosphate, and phosphoric acid, humate, and compost. Deficiency characteristics are weak flower and fruit production.

CARBON is the main energy source in the soil. It is essential for the availability of nitrogen and phosphate and is critical for healthy microorganisms. Between 45 and 56 percent of a plant's compounds contain carbon. Sources of carbon include compost, manures, humates, molasses, organic fertilizers, and coal.

CALCIUM is the king of the nutrients. It is the most critical in low humus soils. Calcium is needed to feed the microbes and affect the permeability of plant cell walls and the thickness of stems. Sources include: lime (calcitic limestone or calcium carbonate), gypsum, marl, and dolomitic lime (which is the worst choice because of magnesium). Deficiency characteristics include die-back of growth tips in tops and roots and increased susceptibility to disease.

HYDROGEN is a nonmetallic element that is the simplest and lightest of all and is one of the three most plentiful elements in plants. It is flammable and the most abundant element in the universe. Hydrogen combines with oxygen to form water (H_2O) and hydrogen peroxide (H_2O_2).

MAGNESIUM has more effect on pH than calcium does. It is important for photosynthesis and helps hold the soil together. Magnesium aids in phosphate metabolism. Plants will show a deficiency if there is too much or too little magnesium. Deficiency will cause thin leaves and yellowing between veins from the bottom of the plant up. Sources include: Sul-Po-Mag, Epsom salts (magnesium sulfate), magnesium oxide, and compost.

POTASSIUM or potash is a metabolic regulator and is essential to the balance between leaf and root growth and necessary for winter and summer hardiness. This element exists in ample quantities in many soils but is often tied up due to mineral imbalance. Sources include: granite, greensand, potassium sulfate, Sul-Po-Mag, molasses, and compost. Deficiency characteristics include early winter-kill, poor survival of perennials, and increased susceptibility to disease.

SULFUR, designated a secondary element, is actually a major element. Like nitrogen, a deficiency causes yellow leaves, but a nitrogen deficiency affects the older leaves first. Sulfur deficiency turns the newest leaves yellow. Sulfur is the easiest leached of all minerals. Sulfur improves the taste of food, increases protein content, and promotes seed production. Sources include compost, molasses, sulfates, elemental sulfur, gypsum, and compost.

CHLORIDE is needed in balanced soils, although excessive amounts can be a great problem in the soil. Sources include city-treated water and compost.

SODIUM has an important relationship with potassium. The available potassium must be higher than the available sodium. Adequate amounts of sodium help to prevent diseases. Sources include most manures, baking soda, organic fertilizers, and compost.

BORON is important for nitrogen efficiency and disease resistance and allows the use of less nitrogen. Deficiencies show up as purple leaves, reduced sugar content, bitter taste, cracks in root crops, and corkiness. Boron exists in all cell membranes and is important for nitrogen fixation.

Boron works closely with calcium and contributes more than any other micronutrient to the quality of produce. Other deficiency symptoms: tip growth dies, light green buds, roots brown in the center, and flowers don't form properly. Boron is also important for disease resistance. Sources include borates, fish meal, and compost. Caution: It is very easy to use too much and cause boron toxicity.

IRON is an essential element for photosynthesis and for the green color in plants. Deficiency shows up as yellow on youngest leaves from top to bottom (veins, margins, and tips stay green). Iron is often tied up in calcareous soils. Sources include copperas (ferrous sulfate), chelated iron, several organic fertilizers, and greensand—especially Texas greensand.

MANGANESE deficiency shows up as white tissue between the veins. Plants will be dwarfed and leaves will have dead spots. If sodium plus potassium equals 10 percent or more of the available nutrients, no manganese will get to the plant. Sources include manganese sulfates, chelates, organic fertilizers, and compost.

COPPER is an important micronutrient for disease resistance. Most soils are deficient in copper. One reason is that too much nitrogen ties up copper. Most common sources are organic fertilizers, seaweed, and compost. Copper sulfate and copper pesticides should not be used.

ZINC availability requires a wellaerated soil and is important for the sweet taste in vegetables and fruit. Deficiency shows in leaves with dead areas, poor bud formation, and small terminal leaves. Weed pressure is greater when zinc is deficient. Sources include kelp meal, liquid seaweed, organic fertilizers, and compost. Synthetic zinc products should not be used.

MOLYBDENUM is important in natural nitrogen fixation but usually unavailable in acid soils. Healthy plants will usually have between .01 and 10 ppm. Other than being important for the health of certain microbes, there is much mystery about the importance of molybdenum. Sources include most all organic fertilizers, humates, and compost.

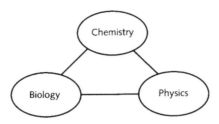

The health, balance, and productivity of the soil depends on three basic pieces being in place: chemistry, biology, and physics. They are all three dependent upon each other. The soil's chemistry must be balanced for the physics and biology to be correct. The living portion of the soil must be healthy for the tilth and drainage to work properly, and the physical properties of the soil must be correct for the living organisms to thrive. Nature will balance the soil for you over time if a few basic ingredients are added and maintained: organic matter, air, and moisture.

HOW PLANTS GROW

Sunlight is the source of all energy. Green leaves are the instruments for gathering in sunlight. Sunlight energy and the gas called carbon dioxide (CO_2) enter the foliage of plants to combine with water and chlorophyll to form sugars, proteins, fats, and carbohydrates—the food stuff of plants. This process is known as photosynthesis. This naturally created food is transferred from the foliage through the stems and limbs down through the trunk into the roots and out into the soil in the form of exudates. Exudates in the form of dead cells and gel-like materials leave the roots through the root hairs and enter the rhizosphere to feed beneficial soil microorganisms.

The rhizosphere is the soil area that is immediately adjacent to the roots. It is the location of the heaviest concentration of microbiotic activity. Some of the beneficial soil microorganisms include: mycorrhizal fungi, nitrogen-fixing bacteria, yeasts, algae, cyanobacteria, actinomycetes, protozoa, mites, beneficial nematodes, and other small animals. Here the roots and soil are working together to produce and release nutrients to feed the plant.

Microorganisms of all sorts feed on the soil's energy-rich substances, releasing a vast array of minerals, vitamins, antibiotics, regulators, enzymes, and other compounds that can be absorbed into the roots and taken back into the plant to produce strong growth and increased pest and disease resistance. Roots take up nutrients from the soil and pass them up into the plant, causing stem and leaf top growth.

Whether the plant is a bluebonnet, bur oak, or bluegrass, the process is the same. This natural process only works at its full potential and efficiency if the soil is healthy. That can only happen in the absence of synthetic fertilizers and toxic chemical pesticides.

HOW TO START AN ORGANIC PROGRAM

The interest and enthusiasm over organic farming, ranching, and gardening is spreading rapidly. My most often-asked question is, "How do I get started?"

Organic agriculture, gardening, and landscaping all have the same basic philosophy of working with Nature's system to maintain the soil, food crops, and ornamental plants without synthetic fertilizers or harsh, chemical pesticides.

Organic fertilizers stimulate soil microorganisms and earthworms, provide humus, and help to aerate the soil. They also provide major nutrients (nitrogen, phosphorus, and potash), as well as secondary nutrients (calcium, sulfur, and magnesium), and many trace elements such as copper, zinc, boron, manganese, and molybdenum. In addition, organic techniques help to save water by allowing soils to drain well while maintaining proper moisture levels for longer periods of time.

Natural organic programs work with Nature's laws and systems rather than try to fight and control Nature as chemical programs do.

I'm reluctant to say it's easy because anything new seems hard at first, especially when a completely new thought process is required. The natural way really is better in every way. Conventional horticulture and ag programs are based on force-feeding plants and killing pests. Organic programs are based on encouraging health and working within Nature's laws to help her control life the natural way.

If you are ready to start your natural organic program, here's how it works.

BASIC ORGANIC PROGRAM

1. SELECT ADAPTED PLANTS - Always use the most well-adapted plants for specific environments. Plant annuals in the proper season and use diversity in your plantings. If you don't use adapted plants, the rest of the rules will do little good.

2. AERATE THE SOIL - Increase the air in the soil through mechanical aeration when needed. Liquid biostimulants and/or living organism products can serve the same function. Use deeply rooted cover crops, encourage earthworms, add compost and mulch to all bare soil. All life needs oxygen and that includes the soil microorganisms. The sticky substance given off by healthy microbes as they break down organic materials glues the soil into a crumb structure creating the perfect air-to-soil ratio.

3. BUILD SOIL ORGANIC CONTENT - Use compost to prepare beds and gardens and apply natural organic fertilizers. Nature has built and maintained fertile soil since the beginning of time in the forests and on prairies through a constant supply of dead plant and animal life as a mulch protecting and composting the soil. Stimulation of microbiotic activity in the soil is the most important way of building soil organic matter. The waste materials and dead bodies of microbes are the specific source.

4. BUILD MINERAL CONTENT - Add finely crushed volcanic rock to all planting beds, lawns, and gardens. Nature has maintained the mineral balance through volcanic eruptions, glaciers movement, and bedrock erosion. Don't worry about pH. When a balance of natural materials is used, pH will move to the correct level. Additional volcanic rock is not needed in volcanic soils. Other kinds of rock minerals can then be useful.

5. MULCH - Nature doesn't allow bare soil and neither should we. For shrubs, trees, and ground covers, use at least 1" of compost and 3" of shredded tree trimmings. Partially completed compost is also an excellent topdressing material. Natural mulch preserves moisture, helps to eliminate weeds, and keeps the soil surface cooler which benefits earthworms, microorganisms, and plant roots.

6. DON'T USE TOXIC POISONS - Do nothing to harm the soil life. There are millions of types of insects and microbes, but only a small percentage are considered harmful; the others are known to be beneficial. Pesticides and harsh synthetic fertilizers hurt or kill both. Two big lies exist and control the industry.

There are two big lies in the horticulture and agriculture industries. These lies have been in power since just after WWII. Before that time gardeners, farmers, and ranchers did a pretty good job of using organic techniques—that's all they had. Yes, even in those days much of the land was "worn out" by overproducing and that mistake caused people to move on to fresh, productive land. The cause was ignorance of the importance of replenishing what is taken away from the soil in the form of crops and what literally vaporizes by tilling and leaving the soil bare. Carbon escapes as carbon dioxide when the land is left bare and tilled too often.

Big Lie Number 1. Plants can't tell the difference between organic and artificial fertilizers. Well, yes, they can. The traditional argument is that plants can only take in fertilizer elements in the basic or ion form. It's a silly notion. These same people will instantly agree that plants take in water—but H_2O is a molecule, not an ion. Plants do not take in H and O ions. To make the example more dramatic, water a white flowering plant with blue, red, or any color dye. The color will move easily into the plant and discolor the flower. Is the dye a basic element or ion? Of course not. It's a very large molecule. One more—herbicides that enter plants and kill by interfering with the normal cellular growth are not ions; they are huge, complex molecules. What do they do, disassemble into carbon, hydrogen, and oxygen, enter the plant, and then reassemble? It would be a funny thought except that this inane comment is often made in total seriousness. Dr. Bargyla Rateaver's books not only explain how plants absorb chunks of materials, including whole bacteria, they have electron microscope photos of the process in action.

There are other differences as well. Organic fertilizers, whether they are meals, manures, or composted plant material, contain N-P-K (nitrogen, phosphorus, potassium), trace minerals, enzymes, vitamins, and lots of organic matter. One hundred percent of each bag's ingredients is useful to the soil and plants. Artificial fertilizers are primarily water soluble mineral salts and phosphorus. There are rarely very many trace minerals included and usually zero organic matter. Some of the synthetic fertilizers have sulfur or polymers to slow down the release process—a move in the right direction, but the organic products have natural slow release.

One more problem. A large percentage of each bag of artificial fertilizers is a mystery. For example, one of the most commonly recommended fertilizers has an analysis of 15–5–10 (the 3–1–2 ratio that's commonly touted). Those numbers stand for nitrogen, phosphorus, and potassium. This particular fertilizer contains 15 percent nitrogen, 5 percent phosphorus, and 10 percent potassium—adds up to 30 percent. Okay, what's the other 70 percent of that bag of fertilizer? Beats me, too. That's the problem. Believe it or not, most states, including Texas, do not regulate the inert ingredients in fertilizers and basically anything can be used including industrial waste and heavy metals. How do you know for sure? Simple—ask the supplier to give you a total analysis. You might notice their knees buckle a little. Although some of the artificial stuff is very clean, I still don't recommend it. Most artificial fertilizers feed plants too fast and a glut of nitrogen causes weak cells and plants that are more susceptible to insects and diseases. Yes, the plants can tell the difference.

The 2nd Big Lie. Toxic chemical pesticides are necessary to control pests and perfectly safe when used according to label directions. I spend my life these days explaining this in detail, but here's the concept in a nutshell. If pesticides worked, this lie might not be so bad. However, there is more money spent today on pesticides than ever before, yet about one-third of all food crops are still lost to pest insects. That's the same percentage as before the pesticides became available. Toxic pesticides kill beneficial insects and beneficial microorganisms. They also damage the frogs, toads, lizards, birds, bats, and other good guys. The irony is that these high-tech pesticides damage the animals that provide powerful natural pest control. Furthermore, healthy soil produces healthy plants that have a natural insect and disease resistance. Adapted plants that are planted in soil full of compost, rock powders, living organisms, and available nutrients are not in stress and don't attract insect pests and pathogenic microorganisms.

7. ENCOURAGE BIODIVERSITY - Encourage life and biodiversity by introducing beneficial insects and protecting those that exist. Plant cover crops and hedgerows. Purchase and release ladybugs, green lacewings, and trichogramma wasps. You'll need to buy less every year because natural populations will establish.

Troublesome insects, diseases, and weeds are symptoms of one of the above rules being violated. Using pesticides only treats the symptoms. Pests are the effects of deeper problems. However, most of the research time and money has been foolishly spent on treating symptoms and ignoring the cause. Don't be one of the foolish.

Please remember that you are dealing with living soil, living plants, and other living creatures. Nature is dynamic and always changing. No program is the best for everyone, so start out with my program and then fine-tune it into your own. No single organic program is perfect—except for Nature's own.

BUILDING A HEALTHY SOIL

Building a healthy soil is done by putting the basic elements in place and letting Mother Nature do the rest. Most unhealthy soils lack air and humus, have a weak population of microorganisms, and are chemically unbalanced. All these things are related, and improving any one of them indirectly improves the others.

The first step in major soil improvement is to aerate the ground. Cultivated and pasture land can be ripped or chisel plowed, and turf areas should be mechanically aerated. Ornamental beds should be aerated with a turning fork or hand aerated. Liquid microorganism products can also be used to increase the oxygen in the soil.

The next step is to have the soil tested. Soil samples may be collected any time. However, *if no samples have been taken on an area within the last two years, the best time to sample is as soon as possible.* Soil testing should be done every year ideally and at the same time of year.

STEPS TO SOIL TESTING

1 **PREPARE A MAP OF THE AREAS TO BE TESTED:** A good map makes your sampling repeatable from year to year and is useful at the time of fertilization. Divide the landscape, field, or pasture into areas where the soil has the same color, slope, surface, texture, internal drainage, and past history of erosion. Each area should have the same plant type (i.e., beds, turf, etc.). Assign each of the areas sampled a letter. For example, Area #1 could have three areas: A—the high ground, B—the sloping ground, and C—the low, level ground. The numbers written on the sample bags would be 1A, 1B, and 1C. As a general rule, any area that is different in slope, texture, color, etc. and large enough to be fertilized separately should also be sampled separately.

2 **COLLECT THE SAMPLE:** Using a soil probe or trowel, push the probe down to plow depth or 6½–7" (4" for no-till, pastures, and lawns). Remove any grass or thatch on top and put the rest of the probing into a soil sample bag or plastic container. Ziplock bags are fine—as long as they have never been used. Do not use paper sacks from the grocery store, bread wrappers, etc. due to possible contamination. Avoid using previously used buckets. Probe the soil every 50 to 100 paces, always taking a minimum of 5 probes per composite sample for small areas, and one probe for every one or two acres from larger areas. Only a small amount of soil is necessary for analysis.

3 **LABEL THE BAGS:** Indicate name and area letters on the sample bag. Make sure the labeling on the bag matches the number of the area on the map it is to represent. It is helpful to label the bags to match the areas before taking the sample. Soils may be sent in dry or wet.

4 **SEND SAMPLES:** Send the samples to a soil testing service that provides organic recommendations. Extension services usually do not provide this service. Tests based only on the pH give no information about what nutrients are available to the plants. Another helpful soil

test is to dig a cubic foot of soil and sift it into a bucket or wheelbarrow. If the sample doesn't contain at least 10 earthworms, do more organic treatments. Use more compost, organic fertilizers, rock powders, sugars, and natural mulches.

Balanced Soil Has Approximately the Following Breakdown.

Oxygen	4–5 percent
Humus	2.5–5.0 percent
Calcium	65–75 percent
Magnesium	12–20 percent
Potassium	3–7.5 percent
Phosphate	250–375 PPM
Sulfate	25–50 PPM
Nitrogen	20–40 PPM
Sodium	0.5–3.0 percent
Salt	400 PPM or less
Chlorides	80–120 PPM
Boron	0.8–2.0 PPM
Iron	200 PPM or more
Manganese	50–125 PPM
Copper	2–5 PPM
Zinc	10–20 PPM

percent = percentage of available nutrients
PPM = parts per million

For soil testing:
Texas Plant and Soil Lab
Edinburg, TX
K. Chandler   956-323-0739

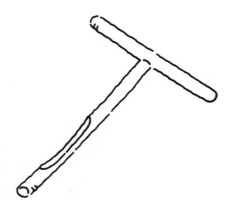

RE-CREATING THE FOREST FLOOR

The next step in becoming organic is to re-create the forest floor in all your beds, vegetable gardens, and ornamental gardens. Pastures and turf also need to have the components of the forest floor.

A natural forest floor cross section looks like this: the top 2–4" is mulch—leaves, twigs, bark, dead plants, dead bodies of animals, and animal manure. Below that is 1–2" of one-year-old organic matter and well-broken-down humus. Below that is a mixture of humus and the rock particles of the area. Minerals are contained in the humus and in the broken-up pieces of the base rock material. Below that is the subsoil. Earthworms, insects, and roots are mixed all throughout the layers. The top 7" of the forest floor is the area that is the most well-aerated and host to the bulk of soil biology. That layered structure, transitioning down from rough mulch to subsoil, is exactly what we want to create in the vegetable garden and in the ornamental garden.

This very definite layering of rough mulch on top of humus and native soil is Nature's way of covering, protecting, and stimulating the soil. Why then should we not do the same thing in our cultivated gardens? Nowhere in the wild will Mother Nature allow the ground to be bare, except for deserts and naturally eroded areas.

There are several ways to create a man-made "forest floor." The easiest way is to take the leaves from your own property or from the plastic bags unenlightened neighbors have left along the street and dump them onto bare areas in the planting beds. The depth of this raw material can range from 8–12 inches. This easy method can also be done with clean hay, tree trimmings mulch, and most any raw organic material. Fine-textured matter such as sawdust, if used at all, should be applied in thinner layers since there is less air space between the small pieces and therefore less oxygen and carbon dioxide exchange at the soil surface. It's better to compost fine-textured materials such as sawdust or other fresh materials before using them on the beds.

A better way to create the "forest floor" is to use partially completed compost. The texture of the material will be better and the resulting improvement to the soil will be faster. Partially completed compost means you can still identify a portion of the raw materials. The texture is better because a mix of large and small particles and decomposed particles will exist. Soil improvement will be faster because of the high population of beneficial microorganisms. I use partially completed compost as mulch at a depth of 4–6."

To go a step farther, apply a layer of completed compost on the bare soil at a depth of 1–2" and cover the compost with a thick blanket (3–6") of shredded native tree trimmings, hardwood bark, pine needles, cypress mulch, or clean hay. Pine bark can be used, but it is my least favorite choice because its flat pieces can plate to seal off oxygen and it can move around easily from wind and water. If pine bark must be used, avoid the fine-textured material and use only large scale bark.

I do not recommend mulches made from paper, plastic, or gravel unless you have no source of natural vegetative materials. Various mulching methods will work to keep the soil temperature and moisture correct, prevent wind and water erosion, and stimulate the life in the soil. Covering the bare soil with mulch is probably the single most important aspect of organic gardening.

Here's the ideal way to replicate the "forest floor."

STEP 1: Aerate by punching holes in the ground.

STEP 2: Spray the soil with compost tea, seaweed, and some biological stimulator. Garrett Juice is the best single product to use.

STEP 3: Apply a light coating of earthworm castings—just enough to barely cover the soil.

STEP 4: Apply a 1" layer of finished compost.

STEP 5: Apply a 4" layer of hardwood bark mulch or shredded natural tree trimmings.

Note: As a precaution, it's wise to avoid piling the mulch up onto the trunks of plants. If the mulch is kept constantly wet, it can girdle trees.

We'll never be able to do as good a job as Mother Nature in creating the forest floor, but we can come pretty close.

BIODIVERSITY

I'm a very lucky person. In 1987 I met a fellow from San Antonio who not only became a friend but introduced me to the organic way of life. Malcolm Beck, a longtime organic gardener and farmer from San Antonio, taught me how to make compost. He also taught me that every living thing will sooner or later die and everything that dies rots and recycles its nutrients and energy back into the soil. On the surface that sounds pretty morbid, doesn't it? In reality it is fundamental to understanding life, Nature, and organics. If dead things didn't rot, this earth would be several thousand feet deep in dead bodies and would be a smelly place indeed. Malcolm taught me that the decaying process returns the dead plants and animals back to the earth and into the raw elements from which they were made. These basic mineral elements in their journey back become the nutrition and vitality to feed the next generation of plants, animals, and man. The decaying process is performed by the billions of little creatures in the soil we call microorganisms or microbes. They will do their job with or without our help. In fact, it is almost impossible to stop them. The microorganisms can turn our once-alive organic waste back into fertilizer for our farms, lawns, and gardens. They can, that is, if they are allowed to do so.

Unfortunately, in most cities, vegetative waste such as leaves, grass clippings and tree trimmings are usually buried in landfills where these life-sustaining nutrients are locked away from air and the natural life, death, and decay cycle. What could have been a great benefit to the fertility and well-being of the soil has become a great problem.

Dead organic material can be managed into a financial and horticultural benefit. All we have to do is protect, encourage, and stimulate microorganisms and friends like beneficial insects, frogs, toads, lizards, snakes, birds, and other critical parts of what we lump together into the term "biodiversity." It's simple. Stop killing the living organisms above, on, and in the soil!

Nature is not a bunch of independent pieces. Nature is a whole. It is a complete whole where everything is related to everything else. Hurting any small part of Nature hurts everything and everyone.

All living organisms die and they all rot, and everything that rots provides food and life for the next phase of life. Your compost pile will show this quite clearly if you just watch.

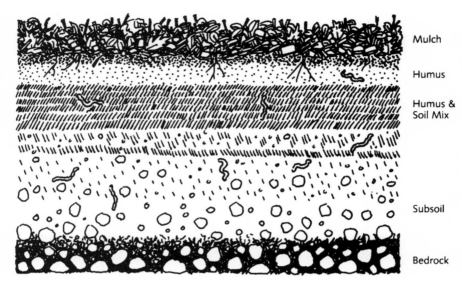

Mulch

Humus

Humus &
Soil Mix

Subsoil

Bedrock

The forest floor soil cross section consists of mulch or litter on the surface, decayed organic matter or humus, followed by minerals and humus mixed, followed by subsoil and bedrock.

PLANT VARIETIES 3

SELECTING ORNAMENTALS

Books exist in most any region of the country that recommend and explain the best plants to use in most any region of the country. Using the native plants of a particular region is becoming more popular and this practice fits together well with an organic program. There are also adapted plants that have been introduced from other parts of the world. I prefer native plants when possible, but the key is to use varieties that will like their new home, making them easy to grow and economical to maintain. In most cases, natives are well adapted and have developed resistance to most harmful insects. Centuries of natural selection have given native plants the ability to survive without pesticides or high levels of fertilization, particularly if they are grown in a healthy soil.

Nature doesn't allow monocultures. Neither should landscape architects or gardeners. When choosing plants (native or introduced), select a variety so that insects and harmful microorganisms will not have one target group. Look at what has happened to millions of American elm trees all over the United States to understand why a diversity of plants is best in the long run. Large monoculture plantings have been devastated.

Another reason to use well-adapted plants in the landscape is water usage and conservation. Water conservation becomes a more serious issue each year and the careful selection of plant materials can make a significant impact on irrigation needs since water requirements vary greatly from plant to plant.

Of course I recommend *Plants of the Metroplex*, *Plants for Texas*, *Texas Organic Vegetable Gardening*, and *Howard Garrett's Texas Organic Gardening* for the Texas area, but similar books exist for other parts of the country. Do yourself a big favor by spending some time at your local bookstore, nursery, library, county agent, urban forester's office, or local college or university, learning about the best plants for your area. Then select a variety of plants that will meet your aesthetic and horticultural needs. In conjunction with the organic practices discussed in this book, you should then have the basics for creating a beautiful landscape, requiring only a minimal amount of maintenance. Note the recommended reading list in the appendix of this book.

My best advice for the selection of trees, shrubs, vines, ground covers, and flowers is to invest in all the local reference books and get the free literature from the botanical gardens, zoos, park departments, and civic garden clubs. Talk to several nurseries, and look at the plants you are considering in different landscape situations. Don't be afraid to try some experiments, but build the framework of the landscape with tough, pest-resistant, adapted varieties.

LANDSCAPING WITH HERBS

Herbs are undergoing a revival. They have been planted for years for their culinary and medicinal uses, but now there's growing interest in another use. Herbs make wonderful landscape plants. Many are drought tolerant and grow in almost any well-drained soil. They provide color, texture, and wonderful fragrances. Herbs also give us help with insect control and make excellent companion plants for our vegetable and ornamental plant materials. They fit perfectly into an organic program because they should only be fertilized with natural fertilizers and they should never be sprayed with pesticides.

There are bush-type herbs such as salvia and rosemary. There are excellent groundcovers like creeping thyme and pennyroyal mint. There are many beautiful flowering varieties such as yarrow and sweet marigold. Herbs also have effective insect controlling qualities. Here are some of my favorite herbs to use as landscape plants. I'm not pooh-poohing the medicinal and culinary uses—quite the contrary—I just like for you to have something else to think about.

BASIL (*Ocimum* spp.) is available in many types of purple and green basil, and they all make excellent annual plants to use as borders or low masses. Plant from seed or transplants in sun or partial shade. They will usually return from seed each year, but if they don't, buy some more.

BORAGE (*Borago officinalis*) is a beautiful, soft herb that grows to about 3 feet tall. The leaves are gray-green and have whitish bristles. The flowers are star shaped and peacock blue and bloom throughout the summer. Plant in sun or partial shade.

CATNIP (*Nepeta cataria*) is a tall ground cover or shrubby perennial with gray-green, oval leaves. It will reach about 3 feet in height. It has small, white or lavender flowers and is excellent for attracting bees and butterflies—and cats, unfortunately. Sun or partial shade.

CHIVES (*Allium schoenoprasum*) grow in clumps and look a little bit like monkey grass. Onion chives have lavender flowers and round leaves. Garlic chives (*A. tuberosum*) have white flowers and flat leaves. Sun or partial shade.

COMFREY (*Symphytum officinale*): The "healing herb" has large, hairy, 10–15" long leaves. The plant will spread to 3 feet high by 3 feet wide and has lovely, bell-shaped flowers in pink and purple shades that hang gracefully from the stems and last throughout most of the summer. It can grow in sun or shade and should be used as an accent plant or in a large massing. Comfrey will stay evergreen during mild winters but always comes back and establishes into a hardy perennial.

DITTANY OF CRETE (*Origanum dictamnus*) is an excellent herb for hanging baskets or patio containers. It has small, soft, round, gray leaves and tiny purple flowers summer through fall. Best in full sun.

GARLIC (*Allium sativum*): Of course, we have to have garlic to ward off the "evil eye" and the bulbs to make the garlic tea, but it is also a good-looking landscape plant. The foliage of garlic is dark green and the flowers are very interesting as they curve around and finally burst open in the early summer. Best in full sun but can take some shade.

SCENTED GERANIUMS (*Pelargonium* spp.) are excellent landscape plants because of the lovely texture and the delicate flowers but more importantly the fragrance when rubbed against or crushed. They come in all sizes and all leaf shapes including deeply cut leaves and those that are soft and velvety. Use in sun to partial shade.

ELDERBERRY (*Sambucus canadensis*) is a large-growing, beautiful perennial that is often grown for its edible purple-black berries in August through September. It can grow to a height of 10–12 feet in most soils and has lovely white flower clusters in the summer. It is also noted for its ability to produce very fine humus soil in the root zone and is a wonderful plant for attracting birds. Sun to partial shade.

GARDEN SAGE (*Salvia officinalis*) is a very tough, evergreen perennial with grayish-green leaves. The only negative is that it will develop woody growth after a while and need to be replaced. There are several different selections including some that have variegated foliage. Plant in sun or partial shade, don't overwater, and cut back once in the later winter or early spring.

LAMB'S EAR (*Stachys byzantina*) is a tough, fuzzy-leafed, gray herb that makes an excellent ground cover to contrast with darker green plants. It can take full sun up to some fairly heavy shade. Lamb's ear's velvet-like foliage and lavender blossoms are delightful to see and to touch.

LEMON BALM (*Melissa officinalis*) is an easy-to-grow, fragrant herb with leaves that are light green and oval with scalloped edges. It has a lemony fragrance and is excellent to interplant among vegetable and landscape plants to look good, help repel pests, and attract bees. Sun or partial shade.

LEMONGRASS (*Cybopogon citratus*): is an herb that looks like pampas grass. It grows to a height of about 3 feet, has a wonderful lemon scent, and is excellent for making tea. Although it rarely flowers, it has a lovely texture for a specimen landscape plant. If it freezes, just plant a new one each year. Best in full sun but can take some shade.

LEMON VERBENA (*Aloysia triphylla*) is a wonderfully fragrant addition to the landscape garden as well as the herb garden. It is sensitive to cold so it's best treated as an annual, although it can be used in a pot and brought indoors during the cold months. Best in full sun.

MEXICAN MINT MARIGOLD (*Tagetes lucida*): (See Sweet marigold).

MINT (*Mentha* spp.) Mints of all kinds make good landscape ground covers but be careful—they all spread aggressively. *Mentha pulegium* is pennyroyal and is a good landscape ground cover and reported to repel fleas. Sun or partial shade.

MULLEIN (*Verbascum thapsus*): Common mullein is a wildflower in Texas and looks like a large version of lamb's ear but is more upright and has larger foliage. It also has yellow, white, or purple flowers depending on the variety. Also called flannel leaf or old man's flannel, mullein is a distinctive specimen plant to use in the garden. Full sun to partial shade.

PERILLA (*Perilla frutescens*) is an easy-to-grow annual with dark burgundy or green leaves. Growth habits are similar to that of coleus or basil. In fact, it looks a great deal like opal basil. However, it can spread aggressively. It can be planted from seed or from transplants and will reseed easily each year. It looks beautiful in contrast with gray plants such as dusty miller, wormwood, or southernwood. Sun or partial shade.

PINEAPPLE SAGE (*Salvia elegans*) has beautiful, red flowers in the late summer or fall. It perennializes in mild winters but should be considered an annual in sun or shade.

ROSEMARY (*Rosmarinus officinalis*) is a beautiful, gray-green shrub that can grow to a height of 4 feet. It will freeze in hard winters but it is worth replanting every year if necessary. Rosemary has a marvelous pinelike fragrance and beautiful light blue flowers. The low-growing groundcover type is *Rosemary prostratus*.

SAFFRON (*Crocus sativus*): The true saffron is an autumn-blooming crocus that resembles ordinary crocus. It has lavender flowers that show in the fall. The saffron food flavor is made from the red-orange stigmas of the plant. It's easy to grow but very labor-intensive to harvest.

SALAD BURNET (*Poterium sanguisorba*) is a compact evergreen herb that will reach 2 feet tall with a rosette shape. The plant provides a pleasant cucumber fragrance and has flowers that form on long stems growing out of the center of the plant. Its lacy, symmetrical shape and nice texture make it a good accent plant. Sun or partial shade.

SOUTHERNWOOD (*Artemisia abrotanum*) has delicate-looking, dusty-gray foliage that emits a lemon scent even when uncrushed but stronger when crushed. Full sun is best.

SWEET MARIGOLD (*Tagetes lucida*) is a substitute for French tarragon and much easier to grow. It has a strong fragrance in the garden and produces a terrific display of yellow-orange blossoms in the late summer and early fall.

TANSY (*Tanacetum vulgare*) is an easy-to-grow, ferny-leafed herb that blooms with yellow, button-like flowers in the late summer to early fall. Crushed or chopped tansy leaves emit a very bitter taste and are an excellent repellent for ants. Sun or partial shade, but best in sun.

THYME (*Thymus vulgaris*) makes an excellent landscape plant, especially the creeping thyme, which makes a beautiful and extremely fragrant groundcover that is particularly effective between stepping stones and on borders. Creeping thyme also works well on retaining walls to flow down over the wall. Full sun is best.

WORMWOOD (*Artemisia* spp.) is another gray-leafed plant that is extremely drought tolerant and is a nice contrast with darker plants. Best in full sun.

YARROW (*Achillea millifolum*) is a very lacy, fern-like evergreen perennial with colorful flowers on tall stalks that bloom in the early summer in white, pinks, and reds. Best in full sun.

Most herbs will do best in well-drained beds made from a mix of compost, rock minerals, and native soil. The best location is full sun in morning and at least some protection from the hot afternoon sun.

It's amazing how old-fashioned things like organics and herbs have come back so strongly. The reason is simple—they work so well.

Herbs also have effective insecticidal qualities. Here are some of my favorites that can be planted among the other vegetable and ornamental plants to help ward off the listed pests.

Herb	Pests Warded Off	Herb	Pests Warded Off
Basil	Flies and mosquitoes	Rosemary	Cabbage moths,
Borage	Tomato worm		beetles, mosquitoes,
Garlic	Aphids, beetles, weevils,		slugs,
	borers, spider mites	Rue	Beetles
Henbit	Most insects	Sage	Moths
Lamium	Potato bugs	Spearmint	Ants, aphids
Marigold	Many insects	Thyme	Cabbage worms and
Nasturtium	Aphids, squash bugs,		many other insects
	white fly	Lavender	Ants
Pennyroyal	Ants, aphids, ticks, fleas	Tansy	Ants
Peppermint	Ants	Onion	Cabbage moths
Garrett Juice	Most insects	Chives	Many fruit-tree and tomato pests

VEGETABLES, FRUITS, NUTS

To make the best selection, it's best to check with the local extension service, local growers and nurseries, and especially local gardeners. Plant a diverse mix of varieties but try to stick with the toughest and best adapted. An excellent source of information will usually be local organic growers and home gardeners. No matter what vegetables you plant, be sure to prepare well-drained and highly organic beds, plant in the proper season, and put a thick mulch layer over all bare soil.

No matter what food crops you decide to try, remember that in most cases these plants are probably not native to your area. For that reason, it's imperative to loosen the soil to provide plenty of oxygen and add lots of compost for additional humus.

Use natural organic fertilizers liberally if the soil is not biologically healthy and chemically balanced. Also add liberal amounts of rock powders and small amounts of sugar. Supplement the soil treatments by spraying regularly with Garrett Juice. Effective rock powders include colloidal phosphate, greensand, granite, and glacial rock dust.

Keep all bare soil mulched at all times, except when new seeds are coming up. Alfalfa hay is the best mulch for vegetable gardens and should be applied 8" thick to allow for settling. Bermuda should be used very carefully. Much of it contains broadleaf herbicides that can damage or kill crops.

The most common recommendation is to water by drip irrigation and avoid wetting the foliage too often. Water infrequently but deeply when needed. I admit to still watering by sprinkling. I like to see where the water is going.

Control insect pests by releasing beneficial insects and by hand removal. Problem infestations can be controlled with various organic products. Check the pest control section starting on page 95 for further details.

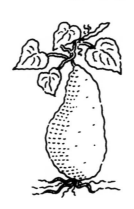

WILDFLOWERS

Wildflowers have always been popular in the wild, at least for those people taking the time to stop for a moment and look at them. On the other hand, many people have become frustrated over trying to establish wildflowers on their own properties. Growing wildflowers can be fairly easy but it isn't as simple as throwing seed on the ground and waiting for the spring show. Once again we need to watch what works in Nature and try to use those techniques and even improve on them where possible.

Here are some tips to help give you a better chance of a beautiful display of wildflower color next spring.

1 **TIMING**: The time to plant is late spring through summer. Sowing the seed in summer best duplicates when Nature scatters seed on the earth. The seed probably need the heat and ultraviolet rays for proper germination.

2 **SOIL PREPARATION:** Begin by raking bare soil to a depth of no more than 1". Deep tilling is not only a waste of money but can actually damage the soil and encourage weeds. If grass or weeds exist in the planting site you've chosen, set the mower on its lowest setting and scalp the area down to bare soil.

3 **PLANTING:** Mist or soak the seed in a 1 percent solution of any bio-stimulant. Next, distribute the seed uniformly over the area at the recommended rate and rake lightly into the soil to ensure good soil/seed contact. It's not essential but is ideal to broadcast a thin (¼") layer of compost over the seeded area. Water the seeded area thoroughly, but be careful to avoid overwatering, which will erode the loose soil and displace the seed. Many of the wildflower varieties will germinate in the fall and the small plants will be visible all winter. Others will only start to be visible the next spring.

4 **MAINTENANCE**: The most critical step in wildflower planting is to help Mother Nature with the watering if needed. Be sure to provide irrigation (it can be temporary irrigation) the first fall if it is a dry season and again in March and April if it's an unusually dry spring. This is a critical step. The tiny plants need moisture as they germinate and start to grow. They will survive in low water settings once established but they need moisture to get started. The only fertilization I recommend is a light application of earthworm castings, compost, humate, or other 100 percent organic fertilizer after the seeds germinate and begin to grow in the early spring. Or, just depend on Mother Nature to take care of things.

5 **SELECTION**: Some wildflowers are easier to grow than others. Here are the ones I would recommend for the beginner. This list will provide a long display and a wide variety of colors.

Wildflower	Scientific Name	Colors
Black-eyed Susan	*(Rudbeckia hirta)*	yellow
Bluebonnet	*(Lupinus texensis)*	blue
Butterfly weed	*(Asclepia tuberosa)*	orange
Coreopsis	*(C. lanceolata)*	yellow
Coreopsis	*(C. tinctoria)*	red & yellow
Cosmos	*(C. bipinatus & C. sulphureus)*	multicolors
Engelmann daisy	*(Engelmannia pinnatifida)*	yellow
Evening primrose	*(Oenothera spp.)*	multicolors
Gayfeather	*(Liatris spp.)*	purple
Horsemint	*(Mondarda citriodora)*	lavender
Indian blanket	*(Gaillardia pulchella)*	red & yellow
Indian paintbrush	*(Castilleja indivisa)*	orange
Indian paintbrush	*(Castilleja purpurea)*	purple
Lemon mint	*(Monarda citriodora)*	purple
Maximilian sunflower	*(Helianthus maximiliani)*	yellow
Mexican hat	*(Ratibida columnaris)*	red & yellow
Ox-eyed daisy	*(Chrysanthemum leucanthemum)*	white
Purple coneflower	*(Echinacea purpurea)*	purple
Snow on the mountain	*(Euphorbia marginata)*	white
Tahoka daisy	*(Machaeranthera tanacetifolia)*	purple
White yarrow	*(Achillea millifolum)*	white
Gold yarrow	*(Achillea filipendulina)*	yellow

PLANTING TECHNIQUES

DRAINAGE

Proper drainage isn't an option— it's a must. If a site doesn't drain, it won't work and plants won't grow properly. Biological activity and chemical exchange will be slowed or stopped; it's that simple. Drainage can be accomplished with surface and/or underground solutions. Any system that works is a good system. There are many organic products that will improve the physical structure and the drainage of any soil, but it's still a great benefit to start any project with proper grading and drainage devices that will get rid of excess water as quickly as possible.

In residential and commercial projects, I recommend and use underground drain lines (perforated PVC pipe) set in gravel for hard-to-drain areas. Using pipe and gravel to drain tree holes can often be the difference between the success and the failure of newly planted plants. A ditch filled with gravel to the soil's surface is an excellent and inexpensive tool to drain water from a low spot. Use no filter fabric.

Liquid biological products can also help improve drainage by stimulating the beneficial organisms in the soil. Garrett Juice can also be helpful.

TREE PLANTING

Trees are the most important landscape element and the only element that actually increases significantly in value after planting. They are the structural features of the landscape and, besides being pleasing to look at and walk under, provide significant services such as blocking undesirable views, shading the ground and other plants, providing protection for wildlife, improving the soil, and providing delightful seasonal beauty.

It is for all these reasons that trees need to be planted correctly so that their root systems develop properly, providing a long, healthy life with a minimum of problems.

Here's how to plant trees organically—The Natural Way.

DIG AN UGLY HOLE: A wide, rough-sided hole should be dug exactly the same depth as the height of the ball but much wider than the ball, especially at the surface of the ground. The width of the bottom of the hole is not important. The sides of the hole should be rough and jagged, never slick or glazed. A saucer shaped hole is good.

RUN A PERK TEST: Fill the hole with water and wait until the next day. If the water level doesn't drop substantially overnight, the tree should be moved to another location, or the drainage must be fixed. Tree planting holes must drain well for proper root development and overall health. Adding a tablespoon of liquid seaweed or Garrett Juice to the perk test water is a good idea. Use about an ounce per 10 gallons of water. This will help the microbial activity to get started in the wall area of the tree hole.

BACKFILL WITH EXISTING SOIL: Backfill only with the soil that came from the hole. Do not add sand, loam, bark, peat moss, compost, or other foreign materials to the backfill. When the hole is dug in solid rock, topsoil from the same area should be used. Some native rock mixed into the soil is beneficial. Topsoil from the immediate area should be used for the to 6–12" of backfill if possible. Remove the burlap from the top of the ball as well as all nylon, plastic string, and even wire mesh. Burlap can be left on the sides and bottom of the ball. Container trees will usually be root-bound. Slash and tear the outer roots away from the ball. This loosening of the roots is a critical step in the planting procedure of container trees but should not be done to ball and burlapped trees. After settling the native soil in the hole with water (not by tamping), cover the surface of the hole with ½–1" of finished compost. Cover the compost with 3–4" of shredded tree trimmings or hardwood bark.

DO NOT WRAP OR STAKE: Wrapping tree trunks is a waste of money, looks unattractive, harbors insects, and leaves the bark weak when removed. Staking and guying is usually unnecessary. If the tree has been planted properly, staking is a waste of money and detrimental to the proper trunk development of the plant. Staking should only be done as a last resort and never left in a place more than one growing season. In areas of the country where sunburn on trunks is a problem, whitewash made from water-based, nontoxic paint is much better than wrapping. As the whitewash wears off, the bark will slowly adjust to the sunlight.

Tree Planting Detail

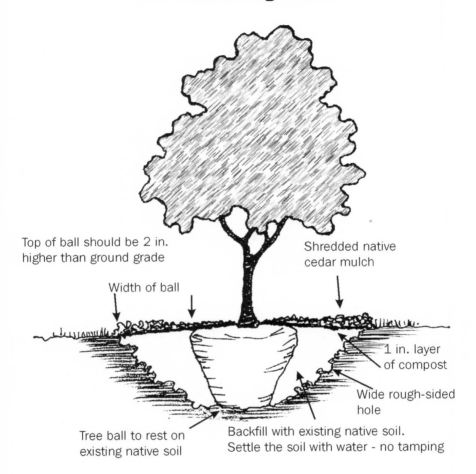

Top of ball should be 2 in. higher than ground grade

Shredded native cedar mulch

Width of ball

1 in. layer of compost

Wide rough-sided hole

Tree ball to rest on existing native soil

Backfill with existing native soil. Settle the soil with water - no tamping

After backfilling:
- Add Volcanite or other volcanic rock dust product to disturbed area at 10 lbs. per 100 sq. ft.
- Add 1″ Compost
- Add 3–5″ native cedar mulch. Do not pile mulch on trucks
- Do not stake trees
- Do not wrap tree trunks
- Do not thin or top trees

Note: Remove any soil that has been added to the top of root balls. Expose the actual top of the root ball.

41

DO NOT OVERPRUNE: It's a serious mistake to think that limb pruning must be done to compensate for the loss of roots during transplanting or planting. Most trees fare much better if all the limbs and foliage are left intact. The more foliage, the more food can be produced to help build the root system. The health of the root system is the key to the overall health of trees. The only trees that seem to respond positively to thinning at the time of transplanting are densely foliated evergreen trees collected from the wild. Plants purchased in containers definitely need no pruning when planted, and no deciduous trees need pruning at planting.

MULCH THE TOP OF THE BALL: Do not plant grass all the way in to the trunk of the tree. Leave the area above the top of the ball unplanted and mulch with 1" of compost and 2–3" shredded tree trimmings or hardwood bark. The compost will act as a slow-release fertilizer as well as a mulch. The reason to avoid grass above the tree ball is to eliminate the competition for water, nutrients, and especially oxygen. As the tree establishes, it's okay for the grass to grow in toward the trunk, although maintaining a mulched area around the trunk of the tree is healthy and helps keep the weed eaters and mowers away from the trunk.

LAWN PLANTING

Lawn planting techniques can be quite simple and economical, or complicated and wasteful. If you follow these simple techniques, your lawn establishment can be successful and affordable.

Soil preparation should include the hand or mechanical removal of all weeds, debris, and rocks over 2" in diameter from the surface of the soil. Rocks within the soil are no problem because they can actually aid drainage. Herbicides are unnecessary and not recommended.

Lightly till or scarify the topsoil to a depth of 2", rake smooth, and gently slope to prevent ponding of water. Deep rototilling is unnecessary and a waste of money unless the soil is heavily compacted. In fact, rototilling can actually damage the soil.

Although the introduction of some organic material can be beneficial, soil amendments in general are unnecessary and only on solid rock areas is the addition of native topsoil needed. Imported foreign topsoil is a waste of money and can cause a perched (trapped) water table and lawn problem. Poor drainage is often a result of this procedure.

Prior to seeding, spray the soil with a biostimulant such as Garrett Juice and treat the seed with one of the same products. Apply a light application of organic fertilizer at the time of the first mowing. Good choices include compost, humate, and earthworm castings.

Severely sloped areas should have an erosion protection material, such as jute mesh, placed on the soil prior to planting. Follow the manufacturer's recommendations for installation.

Some people still recommend the use of toxic herbicides to kill weeds prior to planting. I don't! These chemicals are extremely hazardous and hard on the soil. Use a little more elbow grease and dig the weeds out. The weeds' root system will actually help you establish the permanent grasses.

Seeding and hydromulching should be done so that the seed is placed in direct contact with the soil. If hydromulching is used, the seed should be broadcast onto the bare soil first and then the hydromulch blown on top of the seed. One of the worst mistakes I see in grass planting is mixing the seed in the hydromulch. This causes the seed to germinate in the mulch, suspended above the soil, and many of the seeds are lost from drying out.

After spreading seed, thoroughly soak the ground and lightly water the seeded area as necessary to keep it moist. As the seed germinates, watch for bare spots. Reseed these bare areas immediately. Continue the light watering until the grass has solidly covered the area. At this time begin the regular watering and maintenance program. Deep, infrequent waterings are best. Light watering done every day or every other day causes all kinds of problems, such as shallow roots, salt buildup in the topsoil, and high water bills.

Solid sod blocks should be laid joint to joint after applying a liquid stimulant to the ground. Grading, leveling, and smoothing prior to planting is important. Sod is sometimes rolled with a heavy hand-roller after planting, although compaction from this technique bothers me. The joints between the blocks of sod can be filled with compost or granite sand to give a more finished look to the lawn, but this step is optional.

ORGANIC BED PREPARATION (General)

NEW BEDS WITH NO GRASS OR EXISTING BEDS: No excavation. Add 6" compost, organic fertilizer (2 lbs./100 sq. ft.), rock minerals at 4 lbs./100 sq. ft. and sugar or dry molasses at ½ lb./100 sq. ft., rototill to a total overall depth of 8". Topdress bed with 3" layer of shredded hardwood bark or native tree-trimmings mulch after planting.

NEW BEDS IN GRASS AREA: Remove existing sod with sod cutter or by hand to a depth of 1½", add 4–6" compost, organic fertilizer (2 lbs./100 sq.

ft.), volcanic rock powder at 4 lbs./100 sq. ft., and sugar or dry molasses at ½ lb./100 sq. ft., horticultural cornmeal at 2 lbs./100 sq. ft. rototill to a total depth of 8". Top-dress beds with 3" layer of shredded hardwood bark or native tree-chip mulch after planting.

AZALEA BED PREP: Mix 50 percent shredded hardwood bark or cedar and 50 percent finished compost, 5 gallons of lava sand, and 1 gallon of Texas greensand per cubic yard. Thoroughly moisten the mixture prior to placing in the bed. Excavate 3" and place 15" of the above mix into the beds. The top should be flat and the sides sloped at a 45 degree angle. Mulch with 2" of shredded native cedar.

SHRUB, GROUND COVER, VINE, AND FLOWER PLANTING

Preparing landscape and garden beds correctly the first time allows the plants to establish more quickly, grow faster, and stay healthier. Many people get frustrated with the lack of results and either give up gardening or spend huge sums of money ripping out the plants, preparing the beds correctly, and replanting. So save some time, money, and aggravation by following these steps:

REMOVE WEEDS AND GRASS: Excavate beds to a depth necessary to remove all weeds and grass, including rhizomes. 1½–2" deep is usually enough. Do not use herbicides to kill grass and weeds. Never till first.

ADD TOPSOIL FOR PROPER GRADE: If needed, add native topsoil to all beds to within 2" of the adjacent finished grade. Avoid foreign, unnatural materials, including soils that are different from the existing.

ADD COMPOST: Cover areas to be planted with a 6" depth of properly decomposed and composted organic material. In other words, use compost. Avoid the use of peat moss, raw barks, and other raw materials. Peat moss is ok if you live near a peat moss bog.

ADD ROCK MINERALS: Most soils have plenty of minerals, but in some soil the addition of granite sand, Texas greensand, rock phosphate, lava sand, or other volcanic materials can be beneficial. Soil tests should be made prior to adding these materials. Gypsum is good for soils deficient in sulfur and calcium.

ADD FERTILIZER: An application of an organic fertilizer should be broadcast at 2 lbs./100 sq. ft. onto the planting bed prior to tilling. An application of a biostimulant such as Garrett Juice is also beneficial.

TILL COMPOST TOGETHER WITH NATIVE SOIL: Till the amendments and the existing topsoil together until the compost/soil mixture is 8–10" deep. Ground cover beds do not have to be tilled as deeply.

NEVER TILL WET SOIL: Working wet soil will squeeze the soil particles together, eliminating the air spaces needed for good tilth and soil life.

RAISE THE BEDS: The top of the beds should be flat and higher than surrounding grades with sloped edges for drainage. This lifting happens naturally if proper amounts of amendments are added to the beds.

MOISTEN BEDS BEFORE PLANTING: Planting beds should be moistened before the planting begins. Do not plant in dry soil because the young roots can become dehydrated quickly.

TEAR POT-BOUND ROOTS: Pot-bound plants can resist water and cause the growth of deformed and unhealthy root systems. Cut or tear the mat of circling roots at the outside edge of the root ball, but don't destroy the root system.

WET ROOTS INTO MOIST SOIL: Dip plant balls into water and install sopping wet roots into moist beds.

PLANT THE PLANT LEVEL: Set the plants so that the top of the rootball is even with the surrounding soil. Setting the plant too low may cause drowning and deprivation of oxygen. Planting too high can cause the upper roots to dry out. Quick root development will be aided by spraying the roots of plants with a biostimulant solution such as Garrett Juice before planting.

MULCH BEDS AFTER PLANTING: A minimum 3" layer of organic mulch should be placed on the soil after planting; shredded hardwood bark or native tree trimmings for shrubs and ground cover and a thinner layer of compost for annuals and perennials.

Note: If it sounds simple, it is! Just add plenty of compost and rock minerals into the native soil and mulch all bare soil.

PREPARATION OF FARM LAND

Agricultural land is handled much the same as the home vegetable garden or landscape. It's just that the size is greater, and it's more critical to be as efficient as possible with input costs. Let Nature do as much of the work as possible.

Mechanical aeration and products with low cost per acre such as green manure cover crops, humates, and biological stimulators are important tools.

Compost can be an important tool for farm land. Less-than-finished compost is best for agricultural fields. Compost that has only been turned one time is best so the completion of the composting process happens in the soil. Application should be done, if possible, 6 weeks prior to planting. Compost should be lightly tilled into the soil so that the escaping nitrogen is captured.

Aeration is critical. For tightly compacted soil, use a chisel plow or aerator to break through the hard pan. No till or conservation tillage should be after the first year and plowing should be avoided. Liquid products that can speed up the tilth improvement process include Agrispon, Medina, Bioform, AgriGro, F-68, Bio-Innoculant, and Garrett Juice. Application of dry or liquid molasses will also stimulate microorganisms and increase the natural fertility of the soil.

GARDENING BY THE MOON

People who garden by the moon believe that the same gravitational forces that move the tides up and down also have significant influence on plant growth. Most moon gardeners believe that the increasing light of the moon benefits those plants that bear fruit above the ground. Conversely, they believe that when the moon is on the wane, and its light and gravitational pull are on the decrease, the earth's gravity kicks in again, and the plants that produce below the ground are benefited.

The Old Farmer's Almanac says that flowering bulbs and vegetables that bear crops below ground should be planted during the dark of the moon. That is, from the day after it is full to the day before it is new again. Anything like radishes, onions, potatoes, etc. that grow underneath the ground will grow larger and produce better. If you plant on the new moon, they'll grow tall and bloom, but the veggies won't be good.

Planting should not be done when the moon is absolutely dark because that's when plants should rest. The new moon seems to be a good time to prune and kill weeds because they won't grow back.

Moon gardeners have different opinions, and you can hardly find two who plant exactly the same way. And they all think they're right, because whichever way they choose seems to work.

If you have the time to pay attention to cosmic forces as shown to us by the moon and stars, gardening by the moon can be fun and very productive.

MULCHES

Mulch is a critical ingredient in any organic program. It helps conserve moisture, buffers the soil from temperature extremes, shades out weeds, looks nice, and increases the tilth of the soil. It also supplies food for soil life and nutrients for the soil, keeps raindrops from compacting the soil, keeps the sun from burning the humus out of the soil, and prevents erosion.

After planting any kind of plant—tree, shrub, ground cover, flower, or vegetable—all bare soil should be covered with natural organic mulch. Mulch is not a soil amendment mixed into the soil: It's a covering placed on top of the finished planting bed after the plants have been installed.

Not all mulches are created equal. There are many acceptable mulches but they vary in quality and effectiveness. One of the best topdressing mulches is partially decomposed compost. I discovered the benefit of this material at home as a result of being too impatient to wait on my own compost pile to finish its decomposition. The not-quite-finished compost has larger particles and does a good job of mulching and letting oxygen breathe through to the soil surface and carbon dioxide escape out of the soil to the air.

Grass clippings should only be used as a mulch if mixed with leaves and other debris. I don't recommend lawn grass clippings as a mulch by themselves because the flat blades plate and seal off the soil's gas exchange. Straw and hay can be used if they are free of broadleaf herbicide residue. Alfalfa is the best hay mulch because of its nutrient value and the presence of triacontanol, a growth regulator. Another excellent mulch is shredded hardwood bark. This good-looking material comes from the lumber industry in places like East Texas. It is tree bark that has been run through a hammer mill. This smashing action gives the bark its fibrous texture which helps to hold it in place in your beds even on slopes but still allows air to circulate down to the soil. A less expensive and even better material is shredded native-tree trimmings. They look good and work beautifully. An added benefit of the tree-trimmings mulch is that the buds, leaves, and cambium layer contain protein, which contains nitrogen and other nutrients.

Not all bark makes a good topdressing mulch. For example, the fine to medium grades of pine bark make, at best, a second-rate mulch. Pine bark consists of flat pieces that plate together and seal off the oxygen from the soil. Pine bark often washes or blows away. The tars and resins in pine bark can also inhibit proper aerobic degradation. The only pine bark that makes a decent mulch is the large, nugget size because it will at least stay in place well. The large nuggets don't fit together tightly, so air can still circulate around the pieces down to the soil, and large pieces don't rob nitrogen from the soil as fine-particle mulch sometimes does.

Pine needles are a good choice when used as a topdressing mulch, especially when used in parts of the state where pine trees are native. There's also an economic advantage when the material is locally available and can be gathered from the forest floor, although care should be taken not to deplete the organic matter in any natural setting.

Walnut should not be used as a mulch until fully composted. The raw material has strong growth-retarding properties.

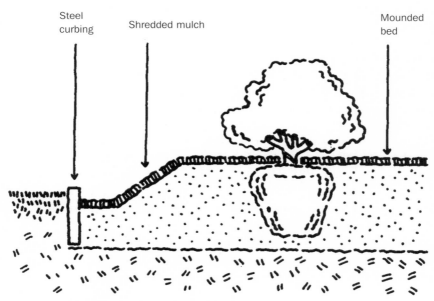

Mulches: To Be Used After Planting. Planting beds should be raised, sloped down on the edge, and covered with a thick blanket of mulch.

Sawdust is sometimes used as a mulch, but I don't recommend it unless it has been mixed with coarser materials and composted for a while. Sawdust does make an excellent ingredient for the compost pile.

Pecan shells make a good topdressing mulch but are much better if composted first with other vegetative materials. Pecan shells are not good to mix into the soil.

Shredded cypress chips make good mulch but tend to mat and seal off oxygen a little more than I would like. They break down very slowly and are more expensive than most other mulches. It's an environmental problem to ship any mulch or compost material great distances.

I do not recommend the artificial mulches such as plastics and fabrics, nor do I recommend gravel as a mulch. The nonorganic mulches don't biodegrade and don't return anything to the soil. Real mulches of organic matter, will eliminate most weeding and cultivation, eliminate soil compaction, save money on irrigation, preserve and stimulate the soil microorganisms and earthworms, and maintain the ideal soil temperature. In the heat of summer, the soil surface under a proper layer of mulch will be around 82–85°. The temperature of bare soil can be in excess of 120°.

Some alleged experts say that whenever a highly carbonaceous mulch such as bark mulch is used, decomposition organisms will steal nitrogen from the soil unless a fertilizer is added that supplies 1 lb. of nitrogen for each 100 lbs. of mulch. Not true! For years I have mulched with hay, bark, tree chips, etc. without supplying extra nitrogen and have never observed any symptoms of nitrogen deficiency as long as the mulch stays on the top of the soil. When raw organic matter is tilled into the soil, there usually is nitrogen draft. Finished compost only should be tilled into the soil. People who still till peat moss and bark into the soil are behind the times.

Conclusion: use compost to prepare planting beds, and use a coarse-textured natural mulch on the surface of the soil after the plants have been installed.

MULCH CHOICES

COMPOST: Compost is an excellent mulch for annuals and perennials and for use as a topdressing mulch for newly planted trees. A light layer of compost is also beneficial on new shrub and groundcover beds prior to the addition of the coarse mulch. Compost is magic! At least it contains Nature's magic. It is also effective to use around sick trees and other plants to help them recover. Compost is Nature's fertilizer. A thin layer of compost is the best choice for young seedlings.

SHREDDED HARDWOOD BARK: Hardwood bark is an excellent mulch material for ornamental planting beds. It is fibrous and has coarse and fine particles, so it grows fungi quickly. The microbes lock the material together to prevent washing and blowing but still allow air transfer to the soil. Hardwood mulch is one of the best choices to use around newly planted trees, shrubs, and other permanent plants. It's also good for potted plants.

CYPRESS CHIPS: Shredded cypress mulch is an acceptable, long-lasting product but more expensive than most other mulch products and the shipping is an environmental problem.

HAY: Hay is good for vegetable gardens. Alfalfa is the best choice— bermuda is the worst because of possible broadleaf herbicide contamination. Layers 8–10" are needed to prevent weed seed germination.

DECO BARK: The large size deco bark is an acceptable mulch to use for shrubs and ground covers. The large size of the deco bark allows air to flow around the large pieces and down to the soil and to the plants' roots.

SHREDDED NATIVE TREE TRIMMINGS: Trimmings are good to use in large areas as a natural ground cover. If ground into smaller pieces, they can be used to mulch all types of plants. Because of the buds and cambium layer under the bark, this mulch contains more nitrogen than most mulches and therefore doesn't take any nitrogen from the soil. Shredded cedar is my favorite of all mulches.

PINE BARK: Pine bark is used widely as a bed preparation material but shouldn't be. Small to medium size bark chips tend to plate together and seal off the soil from oxygen. They also have a tendency to wash and blow away. Very fine particles of mulch can sometimes rob some of the nitrogen from the soil.

PINE NEEDLES: Pine needles are an excellent mulch to use in most planting beds, but they are certainly more appropriate when used in areas where pine trees grow, so they don't look out of place.

SHREDDED NATIVE CEDAR: The best mulch for your property is shredded leaves, tree, and shrub trimmings from plants growing on your property. That simple recycling is Mother Nature's technique. If you have to buy mulch, the best choice by far is native cedar.

"Mulching by itself cannot make up for the shortfall of fertility in the soil."
Dr. William A. Albrecht

"But it can certainly take you in the right direction."
Howard Garrett

Organic Mulches

Organic Mulches	Rating	Application	Remarks
Pine bark (large size)	Fair	3" deep in ornamental beds.	Works well but some people don't like the look.
Pine bark (small to medium)	Bad	Use as a last resort only.	Washes and blows around. Flat pieces tend to seal off oxygen from the soil.
Cedar	Excellent	Shredded cedar is the very best mulch.	Deoiled cedar flakes are the very best greenhouse flooring material.
Coffee grounds	Poor	Best to use in compost pile.	Slightly acid. Will blow and wash away.
Compost	Excellent	Use partially decomposed material 3–5" thick.	Save the more decomposed to till directly in the soil.
Corncobs (ground)	Good	Apply 3" thick.	Availability may be a problem.
Cornstalks (chopped)	Fair	Apply 4–6" deep in vegetable gardens.	Very coarse texture.
Cottonseed hulls	Good	Apply 3–4" deep.	Have fertilizer value similar to cottonseed meal. Very light and tend to blow around.
Cypress chips	Good	Apply 3" deep.	Can seal off oxygen. Expensive.
Lawn clippings	Poor	Better to mix into compost pile.	Good source of nitrogen. Flat pieces plate and seal off oxygen.
Leaves	Good	Best run through a chipper before applying 3" deep.	Blowing and washing can be a problem.
Manure	Fair	Apply only after composting.	Fresh manure can burn plants and can contain weed seeds.

Organic Mulches, Continued

Organic Mulches	Rating	Application	Remarks
Pecan shells, Peanut shells, Rice hulls	Good	Apply 3" deep. Better to compost first with other materials.	Inexpensive, becoming more available, high in nitrogen.
Peat moss	Terrible	Don't use; the worst mulch choice.	Expensive, blows and washes away.
Pine needles	Excellent	Apply 3–5" thick on vegetable gardens and ornamental beds.	Looks best when used in association with pine trees.
Sawdust	Poor	Use in the compost pile, not as a mulch.	Small pieces seal off oxygen exchange when used as a mulch.
Seaweed	Fair	Not readily available but works well.	Watch for salt content. Decomposes slowly.
Straw, hay	Good	Apply 4–5" deep in ornamental beds, 8–10" deep in vegetable garden.	Use for winter protection. Alfalfa is the best. Bermuda grass is the worst because of possible chemical contamination.
Shredded hardwood bark	Excellent	Apply 3–4" deep in ornamental beds.	Best mulch of all for use on sloped areas.
Shredded native tree trimmings	Excellent	Apply 3–4" deep in ornamental beds.	Almost as good as hardwood but cheaper. Cedar is the best.
Gravel	Poor	Best used at 3–6" in utility areas.	Large, decorative stones are good for use in shady landcape areas.
Lava rock	Fair	Apply 3–5" deep too harsh.	Avoid using in large areas—
Shredded native Cedar	Excellent	Apply 3-4" deep around all plantings	Use a thinner layer around vegetables, small flowers, and native plants that have low water requirements.

MAINTENANCE

NATURAL TREE CARE
PRUNING

Is it time to thin my trees and cut off the lower limbs? My answers to these common questions such as this one might surprise you. There seems to be an abundance of curious tree-pruning advice still around. Let's try to straighten it out.

Pruning too much is the most common mistake. Few trees need major pruning every year. Other than some fruit trees, few trees need annual thinning and, unless lower limbs are a physical problem, they should be left on the tree.

TIMING: Landscape trees can be pruned any time of the year, but the best time is from fall to late winter. Fruit trees should be pruned from midwinter up until bud break. Certain fruit trees like peach trees, for example, should only be pruned just before bud break because pruning induces bud break and flowering. Early flowers plus late freezes equals no fruit.

AMOUNT OF PRUNING: Pruning trees is part science and part art. Don't try to change the character and overall, long-term shape of a tree, and don't remove lower limbs to raise the canopy. Low growing limbs exist for a reason. It's very unnatural to strip tree trunks bare. If you think that looks good, think again. Remove dead, diseased, broken, or damaged limbs and the weakest of crossing limbs. Remove limbs that grow toward the center of the tree and limbs that are dangerous or physically interfere with buildings or activities. Thinning to eliminate a certain percentage of the foliage is usually a mistake. Heavy thinning of a tree's canopy throws the plant out of balance, inviting wind and ice storm damage. The resulting stress attracts diseases and insect pests. Gutting is never appropriate.

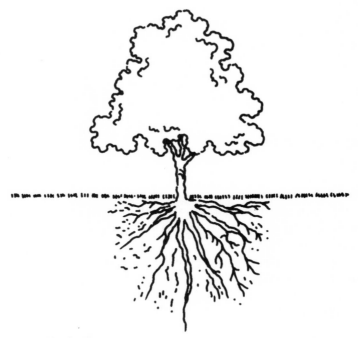

How people think tree roots grow.

How tree roots really grow.

PRUNING CUTS: Pruning cuts should be made with sharp tools. Hand tools such as bow saws, Japanese pruning saws, loppers, and pole pruners are good for small limbs. Chain saws can be used for larger limbs, but only with great care and a thorough understanding of the equipment.

Flush cuts should be avoided. Cuts leaving a ¹⁄₁₆" stub are also bad. Pruning cuts should be made at the point where the branch meets the trunk, just outside the branch collar. The branch collar stub will be ⅛–¼" on small limbs but can be several inches wide on large limbs. It will also be wider at the bottom of the limb than at the top.

It's scientific fact that cutting into or removing the branch collar causes problems. Flush cuts create large, oval-shaped wounds and encourage decay. They also destroy the natural protective zone between the trunk and the branch and can cause several serious tree problems including discolored wood, decayed wood, wet wood, resin pockets, cracks, sun injury, cankers, and slowed growth of new wood. Proper cuts are round, smaller, and heal much faster. Peach, plum, apricot, and other fruit trees are particularly sensitive to flush cuts. Many fruit tree insects and disease problems are related to improper pruning cuts. Long branch stubs are also detrimental and should be avoided.

WOUND DRESSINGS: Research by Alex Shigo, Carl Whitcomb, and the U.S. Forest Service has shown that pruning paint and wound dressings have no benefit and can be harmful by slowing the healing process. Healthy tissue needed for callus formation can be damaged or killed by pruning paint or dressings. Trees have defense cells, much like white blood cells in mammals. These lignin cells are produced on the backside of a wound to naturally prevent diseases from entering fresh cuts. Just as a cut finger heals faster when exposed to the air, so does a tree wound.

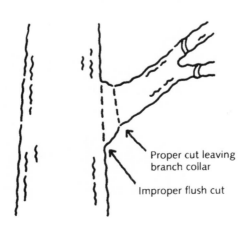

Proper cut leaving branch collar

Improper flush cut

CAVITIES: Cavities in trees are voids where fungi have rotted healthy material. They are usually the result of physical injury. Removing only the decayed material is the remedy. Fillers such as concrete and foam are only cosmetic and not recommended. When removing decayed matter from cavities, be careful not to cut or punch into the living tissue. Injuries to healthy tissue can introduce further decay into the healthy wood. When cavities hold water, drain tubes are sometimes inserted to release water. Bad idea. Drain tubes puncture the protective barriers between the rotted and healthy wood and allow decay to expand. I also don't recommend any of the trunk injector systems for fertilizer and insect control because of their puncture wounds, plus they miss the main problems in the soil and root system. See *Fertilizing*.

CABLING: Weak crotches between limbs can sometimes be stopped from splitting by installing cables horizontal to the ground so the natural movement of the tree is not completely stopped. Cabling used to hold up low-growing limbs is poor tree care and a waste of money. Cabling can be very dangerous and should only be done by professional arborists.

As a final note, the tree trimmings and sawdust resulting from pruning should not be hauled away. The large pieces should be used for firewood and the limbs and foliage should be shredded and used as mulch under trees or mixed into a compost pile.

FERTILIZING: Since all plants require food, trees should not be overlooked when a landscape is fertilized. The easiest way to fertilize trees is in conjunction with the general fertilization of the grass and planting beds beneath the trees. The feeder roots are near the surface, and the tree will utilize whatever nutrients are there. Remember that over 80 percent of a tree's root system is in the top 12–18" of soil.

Putting fertilizer in holes drilled throughout the root zone is not a good idea for general fertilization, but is effective for a specific deficiency such as chlorosis. The roots will take the pure material (sulfur, iron, or magnesium, for example) away from the cores as needed.

A good balanced, organic fertilizer is perfect for establishing a healthy condition for trees. Fertilizer should be applied two or three times a year, as with other plantings. Placing a layer of compost over the entire root zone of the tree (and beyond) will also help greatly to feed the soil and thus the tree. Healthy plants will repel insects and diseases, reducing or eliminating the need for pest control products. Periodic applications of foliar food are also beneficial. The best foliar feeding recipe is Garrett Juice. See appendix for the formula.

AERATION: Mechanical hole punching is recommended for tree care, especially in clay or other heavy soils. Oxygen is one of the most important elements in healthy soil. Air penetration helps greatly to stimulate microbial activity and root growth.

PEST CONTROL: Occasionally trees need to be sprayed to control certain pests, or to give them a little extra nutrient punch. In an organic program, this can be accomplished in one step, reducing the cost once again. Garrett Juice is the best tool. It will indirectly help control most harmful insects without killing the beneficial ones. At the same time, the natural ingredients found in the products act as a foliar fertilizer for the tree. Garrett Juice helps with pest control by improving the immune system of the plants and by feeding and stimulating beneficial microorganisms. When orange oil or d-limonene is added at 2 ounces per gallon of spray, it actually kills pests. See appendix for formula.

The most persistent pest is the aphid, which is the most prevalent in the spring when trees start their active growth cycle. Aphids damage plants by sucking the juices from tender, new growth. There is a very easy way to control aphids—spray with garlic/pepper tea, or sugar water. A water blast followed by the release of ladybugs is my favorite aphid control.

Protecting and adding to the beneficial insect population will give effective control of aphids and other harmful insects. Good insects include spiders, ladybugs, green lacewings, praying mantises, wasps, mud daubers, and others.

Taking care of trees using common-sense techniques and safe products is easy and cost effective. The results are better than using toxic chemical treatments, which will destroy many beneficial insects while only reducing a percentage of the target insects. Imagine being able to spray trees without worrying about wind drift, lawsuits, overapplication of material, and the real possibility that the environment is being harmed each time a pesticide is applied. That's the beauty of tree care using the natural approach—it is safer and it works!

LAWN CARE

Grass is the most intensely maintained of all plants and indeed the biggest expense in any landscape maintenance budget. It is scalped, mowed, fertilized, sprayed before weeds appear, sprayed after weeds appear, walked on, driven on, and usually abused all during the year. As with all plant types, there are some cost effective, organic approaches for the natural care of grasses.

MOWING: Many turf areas are mowed too low. When grass is mowed short, the root system is correspondingly too short. That increases the demand for water and food, encourages weeds to germinate, and can cause the lawn to decline.

Generally, turf should be mowed to a height of at least 2½" or taller and should not be allowed to grow taller than ⅓ again its height between mowings. Cutting more than ⅓ of the grass blades can cause noticeable damage to the grass, which can take several days to overcome. Golf courses and other playing field turf areas don't always have the luxury of letting the grass grow taller but landscape areas certainly do.

Another important mowing technique is to leave the grass clippings on the ground—don't bag them and haul them away. This practice wastes time and money and is detrimental to the lawn. There's also an environmental issue related to the crowded condition of municipal landfills. Grass clippings in plastic bags have been responsible for a large percentage of the waste in city dumps.

Grass clippings left on the lawn will decompose rapidly in the presence of water and organic fertilizer, creating food for microbes and the much-needed humus for the soil. Since the organic matter makes the soil healthier, the number of weeds will be reduced. Discarding the grass clippings also throws nutrients away. Tests at the University of Connecticut agricultural experiment station showed, through the use of radioactive isotopes, that nitrogen in grass clippings left on the lawn was back in the growing plants in as short a time as one week.

Scalping a lawn in the spring is a waste of time and money. It is also harmful to the lawn. When the soil is exposed through scalping, humus is burned out of the soil, microbes suffer, and weed seeds germinate.

AERATION: Aerating the soil is an important procedure in establishing soil health and going "organic." Soil will naturally become aerated by the addition of humus and the stimulation of earthworms and microbial activity if given enough time. All you have to do is add compost and organic fertilizers and stop using harsh, synthetic products, and Nature will take over.

However, most of us want the process to go faster, and the answer is "punching holes" in the ground. These holes can be punched with a stiff-tined turning fork or any spiked tool. The most convenient method is to buy or rent an aerator or hire a landscape contractor to use a mechanical aerator to poke holes all over the yard. Hand work usually has to be done in the beds.

Mechanical aerators are available in all shapes and sizes with many features. Some just punch small holes, others remove cores, and some inject water while punching holes. Some can even punch holes 12" deep. All these machines work. The more holes, the better, and the deeper the holes, the better. Just choose a machine that fits your budget, because the cost ranges greatly. The object is getting oxygen into the soil. When that happens, microbe populations start to increase instantly, natural nitrogen cycles function properly, and Nature's wonderful systems are all set in motion. It's not necessary to understand all the systems in great detail—but it's only important to respect their presence and let them work for you.

FERTILIZING LAWNS: Another tip for good organic lawn care is to avoid chemical fertilizers, which are usually applied three, four, or more times a year. They green up a lawn quickly, but their effect soon falls off as the chemicals are leached out of the soil or washed down the street. Besides, they create a major hardship for the poor guy or gal who's pushing the mower because chemical fertilizers create flushes of heavy growth. Chemical fertilizers feed the plants artificially and do nothing for the soil, so their long-term effect is quite damaging.

Organic fertilizers provide the proper nutrients without damaging the soil. Natural fertilizers only need to be applied two or three times a year, and are safe, and don't leach away. They release nutrients slowly,

feeding the plants only what they need and at the proper time. The result is green, healthy grass with slower, more consistent growth, making it easier to avoid having to catch the grass clippings.

Supplemental feeding of a lawn can be done at any time using liquid foliar spray such as Garrett Juice. Foliar feeding will prevent the yellow, chlorotic look that lawns often have in late summer when the hot, dry days take their toll. It can also be used on grass areas any time to give the color a boost. Foliar feeding can reduce stress damage and improve cold tolerance. Liquid seaweed is an important ingredient in any spray program.

PEST CONTROL: The next lawn care necessity is spraying for all the things that don't belong. Most of the harmful insects, fungi, and bacteria can be controlled with beneficial nematodes and cornmeal. A healthy soil that drains well is the best long-term control.

Weeds can be controlled with organic products. Building a healthy soil, applying adequate fertilizer and water, and mowing on time will prevent most weeds, but there are no nontoxic herbicides on the market today that are foolproof. The only foolproof method of safely eliminating weeds is hand pulling or mechanical devices. An organic herbicide can be made by mixing 1 cup of orange oil and 1 cup of molasses into 1 gallon of 20 percent vinegar.

COMPOSTING LAWNS: Composting helps both in fertilization and weed control. A ¼–1" layer of compost spread over a lawn once a year will provide the grass most of the nutrients it needs. It is an expensive process compared to cheap chemical fertilizers, but it improves the health of the soil and grass and will act as a buffer to extreme climatic changes and even to harsh chemicals. When funds are limited, composting every other year will usually be adequate. This isn't needed any longer once the soil is healthy.

Compost will also help prevent weeds by increasing the health of the soil. Few noxious weeds will grow in a healthy, balanced soil, and what few do appear are easily removed by hand or spot spraying. Learning to accept a lawn with a mix of grasses, wildflowers, and herbs is not only okay but recommended.

Safe lawn care is critical because the lawn is where the most people-use occurs, and the absence of chemicals means a healthier environment for children, pets, and others. Children are a very special concern but the elderly and ill people of all ages are also particularly sensitive.

RENOVATING A WORN OUT LAWN: For compacted, weedy, unhealthy lawn areas: First, mechanically aerate and don't be bashful—tear up the ground. Next, spray the area with Garrett Juice. Next, apply an organic fertilizer at 20 lbs./1,000 sq. ft. For additional help, add ¼" of compost, which is about 1 cubic yard per 1,300 sq. ft.

SHRUB, GROUND COVER, VINE, AND FLOWER CARE

Shrubs, ground covers, flowers, and vines are the easiest plants to maintain. Sometimes they need light pruning, fertilizing, and even spraying, but they are easily accessible (unlike trees), and, unlike grass, do not require intense maintenance.

PRUNING: Pruning shrubs, ground covers, and perennial flowers is really quite simple. Remove only enough growth to keep the plants under control. For example, most ground covers will need to be pruned back once in the early spring to remove the dead stubble, and after that only when they encroach on paved surfaces or other planting areas.

Perennials should be pruned in the late fall or winter to remove the previous year's dead growth. Or, prune in the season opposite the bloom period. For example, prune spring-blooming perennials in the fall and fall-blooming perennials in the spring. Additional heavy pruning after strong flushes of flowers have started to play out will often promote a new flush of flowers.

Shrubs will need more frequent pruning to keep them under control. Light, selective pruning is the best technique. Never prune shrubs by removing a large amount of growth or by constantly "boxing" them, which removes the new growth. Not only does it make the shrub look artificial, it will ultimately ruin the usefulness of the plant and weaken the plant by reducing the photosynthetic surface. The exception here, of course, is a formal garden, which does require clipped hedges.

FERTILIZING: As with trees and lawns, landscape beds should be fed with organic fertilizers two or three times a year. Flowers will usually need supplemental fertilizers like bat guano, blood meal, fish meal, or manufactured organic fertilizers. A Garrett Juice drench of the soil is also helpful.

PEST CONTROL: As a general rule, spraying to kill insects is not necessary and should not be done by the calendar or on a preventative basis, but instead at the first sign of infestation. For example, the annual ritual of applying insecticides in August for grubworms is one of the most blatant wastes of money and sources of pollution in landscape maintenance. Grubs are only damaging enough to treat when 8–10 per sq. ft. are found. Most grubworms are actually beneficial. Work to improve the soil through aeration and organic fertilizers; use beneficial insects regularly and the least toxic pesticides as a last resort.

COMPOSTING: Compost should be used around shrubs, ground covers, and flowers to help increase soil health, moisture retention, climate buffering, and weed control. Whenever compost is used as a mulch, it should be spread to a minimum 2" depth. Once the ground is covered with plant growth, a light (½") application of compost annually is all that's needed.

INTERIOR PLANTS: Interior plants should be planted in well-drained, organic soil. The soil should not be sterile, but alive with microorganisms and earthworms. Some of the best fertilizers for interior plants include earthworm castings and kelp meal. They are mild and odor free. Volcanic rock such as lava sand should also be used.

Pests on interior plants are best controlled by using liquid seaweed, Neem, garlic tea, and biostimulants. Horticultural oil products can be used for severe problems.

For success, give your interior plants plenty of light, moderate amounts of water and fertilization, and a gentle misting of water regularly. If your water is alkaline, add 1 tablespoon of apple cider vinegar to each gallon of water.

Organic maintenance is really just a matter of copying what Nature does when left alone—it allows only adaptable plants to survive, strives to keep the ground covered, and utilizes organic matter in a never-ending cycle. Man has disrupted that cycle over the years, but by using common sense and safe products, the delicate balance can be reestablished. Patterning any landscape maintenance program after Nature's own cycles will go a long way toward repairing the damage that has been done and will grow more beautiful plants than you ever imagined.

BASIC ANIMAL CARE

COOKING FOR YOUR PETS

> **Healthy Pet Diet For Dogs**
>
> - 50 percent grain (rice, barley, etc.)
> - 25 percent meat (rabbit, chicken, etc.)
> - 25 percent veggies (steamed)
> - 2 percent natural diatomaceous earth
> - ⅛ tsp. food grade kelp (daily)

> **Healthy Pet Diet for Cats**
>
> - 50 percent meat
> - 25 percent grain
> - 25 percent veggies (steamed)
> - 2 percent natural diatomaceous earth
> - ⅛ tsp. food grade kelp (daily)

COMMERCIAL PET FOOD:
If you don't like to cook for your pets, buy and feed dogs and cats Muenster Natural Pet Foods. For information call 800–772–7178.

PET FOOD ADDITIVE: For extra help in improving pets' immune systems, give animals the Missing Link. For information call 800-615-0031.

Don't forget to brush, bathe, and exercise your pets regularly!

SEVEN STEPS IN GOING ORGANIC

The basics of organics is soil improvement. Healthy soil produces healthy plants with very powerful natural insect and disease resistance.

1 Stop catching the grass clippings. Allow the clippings to return to the soil.

2 Stop using synthetic fertilizers and synthetic pesticides.

3 Start using compost, volcanic rock powders, and natural fertilizers.

4 Use natural or least toxic pesticides, but only when needed for specific pests.

5 Select native and well-adapted plants and plant at the correct time of year.

6 Mulch all bare soil—a must!

7 Water thoroughly and deeply, but less frequently.

MAKING COMPOST

Compost is a living fertilizer that can be made at home or purchased ready to use. A compost pile can be started at any time of the year. Good ingredients include leaves, hay, grass clippings, tree trimmings, food scraps, dead animals, bark, sawdust, rice hulls, weeds, spoiled food, nut hulls, animal manure, and anything else that was once alive. Mix the ingredients together in a container of wood, hay bales, hog wire, or concrete blocks, or simply pile the material on the ground.

The ideal mixture is 80 percent vegetative matter and 20 percent animal waste, although any mix will compost. The ingredients should be a mix of coarse and fine-textured material. Avoid having all the pieces of material the same size since the variety of sizes will help air to move through the pile. Oxygen is a critical ingredient.

Try to turn the pile at least once a month; more often speeds up the process. Keep the pile moist, roughly the moisture of a squeezed-out sponge, to help the living microorganisms thrive and work their magic. If you never turn the pile, it will still compost.

Compost is ready to use when the ingredients are no longer identifiable. The color will be dark brown, the texture soft and crumbly, and the aroma that of a forest floor. Use compost in all bed preparation and as a high-quality mulch around annuals and perennials.

COMPOST LOCATION: anywhere, sun or shade ; on soil or concrete.

COMPOST INGREDIENTS: anything that was alive.

COMPOST TEA: soak manure compost in water for 3-14 days until a dark liquid is formed. Aerating the brew with a simple aquarium pump creates a more beneficial microbial population in the tea. Add 1-2 oz. of molasses per bucket of tea along with a handful of comfrey leaves or blackberry leaves. Dilute the concentrated tea to iced tea color for spraying plants.

MONTHLY ORGANIC MAINTENANCE CALENDAR
JANUARY

PLANT:*
- Fruit and pecan trees, grapes, berries, asparagus, onions, potatoes, English peas, anemones, & ranunculus.
- Shrubs, vines, balled-and-burlapped or containerized trees.
- Spring flowers and vegetable seeds indoors.
- Complete tulip, daffodil plantings in early January. "Force" bulbs in pots indoors.
- Cold-hardy color: dianthus, pansies, flowering kale, and cabbage (if the weather is mild).
- Transplant plants during dormant period.

FERTILIZE:
- Garrett Juice as a root stimulator to new shrubs and trees, monthly until plants are established.
- Asparagus beds in late January with manure-based fertilizer.

PRUNE:
- Shade trees by removing dead and damaged limbs.
- Summer-flowering trees, including crepe myrtles, by removing no twigs larger than a pencil in diameter.
- Evergreen shrubs if needed.
- Fruit trees. However, the best time is just before bud break in late winter.

WATER:
- Spot-water any dry areas to avoid plant desiccation.

PEST CONTROL:
- Apply horticultural oil if needed to scale-prone plants such as: oaks, hollies, camellias, euonymus, pecan, and fruit trees. Remember that organic pesticides kill good bugs as well as pests.
- Houseplants: To control pests such as mealybugs, spider mites, and scale, spray with biostimulant, liquid seaweed, and mild soap mixture. Apply horticultural cornmeal to the soil.

ODD JOBS:
- Have soil tests run.
- Turn compost pile monthly or more often and keep moist.
- Plan spring landscape improvement projects and begin construction activities.
- Prepare garden soil by adding compost and volcanic rock, and mulching bare soil. Take mower, tiller, trimmers into shop for repairs before spring.
- Feed and water the birds!

*Planting recommendations based on North Texas climate. Check with your local nurseries and extension service for specific varieties and timing in your area.

FEBRUARY

PLANT:*
- Broccoli, brussels sprouts, cabbage, cauliflower, onions, English peas, asparagus, potatoes, other cold-tolerant vegetables, and strawberries for harvest next spring.
- Petunias, pansies, pinks, snapdragons, alyssum, calendulas, glads, cannas, and daylilies.
- Fruit trees and berries.
- Transplant existing landscape plants.
- Transplant crowded summer-blooming perennials.

FERTILIZE:
- All planting areas with a natural organic fertilizer at approximately 20 lbs./1,000 sq. ft. If the soil is already healthy, the rate can be reduced to 10 lbs./1,000 sq. ft.
- Cool-season flowers with earthworm castings, fish meal, and bat guano at 10 lbs./1,000 sq. ft.
- Spray growing plants with Garrett Juice.

PRUNE:
- Shade and ornamental trees lightly to remove dead, diseased, and crossing limbs.
- Peaches and plums by 40–50 percent to encourage 45° angle growth; grapes, by 80–90 percent. Other fruit trees as needed. Pecans need little to no pruning.
- Evergreens and summer-flowering plants.
- Bush-form roses (not climbers).
- Winter-damaged foliage from liriope, ophiopogon, honeysuckle, Asian jasmine, and other ground covers.

WATER:
- Winter annuals and dry soil areas as needed.

PEST CONTROL:
- Giant bark aphids: no treatment needed in most cases.
- Horticultural oil for serious infestations of scale insects. Be sure to keep mixture shaken while using and follow label instructions carefully. Use sparingly if at all. Apply beneficial nematodes to help control grubworms, fleas, fire ants, and other pests.

ODD JOBS:
- Adjust and repair sprinkler system.
- Have soil tested. Watch for accumulations of phosphorus.
- Have maintenance equipment repaired for spring use. Sharpen hoes, pruning tools, and mower blades.
- Add compost and topdressing mulch to all unhealthy soil areas.
- Turn the compost pile regularly.
- Feed and water the birds!

Planting recommendations based on North Texas climate. Check with your local nurseries and extension service for specific varieties and timing in your area.

MARCH

PLANT:*
- Trees and shrubs.
- Finish cool-season vegetable plantings. See February and April. Begin warm-season crops after last killing freeze date.
- Summer herbs: lemongrass, lemon verbena, thyme, lavender, salad burnet, mint, oregano, sage, etc.
- Plant a mixture of varieties and include some open-pollinated choices.
- Continue to plant cool-season annuals such as petunias and snapdragons. Begin planting warm-season types after last killing freeze.

FERTILIZE:
- All planting areas with a natural organic fertilizer at approximately 20 lbs./1,000 sq. ft. (if not done in February).
- Spray all growing plants with Garrett Juice.

PRUNE:
- Spring-flowering shrubs and vines only after they finish blooming: flowering quince, spirea, forsythia, weigela, azaleas, camellias, Carolina jessamine, wisteria, lady banksia rose, etc.
- Fruit trees just before bud break.

WATER:
- Annuals and other dry soil areas as needed.
- Wildflower areas in dry years.

PEST CONTROL:
- Loopers and caterpillars: *Bacillus thuringiensis* (Bt) biological worm spray. Release trichogramma wasps.
- Pillbugs, snails, slugs: Garlic-pepper tea, beer traps, and dust around plants with a mix of hot pepper, natural diatomaceous earth, and cedar flakes.
- Aphids: A blast of water and a release of ladybugs. Add 2 ounces molasses per gallon for better results.
- Black spot, powdery mildew, bacterial leaf spot: Garrett Juice plus a cup of skim milk per gallon of spray.
- Sycamore anthracnose: Bordeaux mixture as leaves emerge. Perform Sick Tree Treatment as needed; see appendix.
- Fruit trees: Spray Garrett Juice plus garlic tea at pink bud and again after flowers have fallen from the trees. Spray Garrett Juice only every two weeks.

ODD JOBS:
- Turn the compost pile.
- Use completed compost for bed preparation. Use partially completed compost or shredded native as a topdressing mulch.
- Mulch all bare soil.
- Feed and water the birds!

Planting recommendations based on North Texas climate. Check with your local nurseries and extension service for specific varieties and timing in your area.

APRIL

PLANT:*
- Turfgrass from plugs, sod, sprigs, or seed.
- Roses from containers.
- Container-grown fruit and pecan trees.
- Warm-season flowers, including: (for sun) periwinkles, cosmos, portulaca, copper leaf begonias, marigolds, zinnias, lantana; (for shade) caladiums, coleus, begonias, impatiens, and nicotiana.
- Summer herbs: continue to plant.
- Warm-season vegetables, including melons, okra, southern peas, corn, squash, beans, cucumbers, eggplant, and tomatoes.
- Summer/fall-flowering perennials.
- Herb-garden plants in beds, pots, and hanging baskets.

FERTILIZE:
- Summer-flowering shrubs and roses.
- Spray all plant foliage with Garrett Juice. Add garlic tea if minor insect or disease problems exist.
- Apply Garrett Juice to the soil as a root stimulator monthly to newly planted trees and shrubs.

PRUNE:
- Spring-blooming vines and shrubs immediately after bloom.
- Pick-prune hedges to be wider at the bottom for better light and thicker growth.

WATER:
- All planting areas deeply but infrequently during dry periods.
- Potted plants as needed. Add 1 ounce of Garrett Juice per gallon of water.

PEST CONTROL:
- Release green lacewings for control of thrips in roses, glads, other flowers.
- Snails, slugs, pillbugs: Spray garlic-pepper tea, use beer traps, or dust around plants with cedar flakes, hot pepper, and natural diatomaceous earth.
- Release trichogramma wasps for pecan casebearers.
- Ticks, fleas, and chiggers: natural diatomaceous earth when weather is dry and apply beneficial nematodes anytime.
- Treat peaches and plums and other fruit with the Organic Fruit and Pecan Tree Program. See appendix.
- Aphids: water blast followed by release of ladybugs. Add 1–2 oz. of molasses for better results.
- Black spot on roses: Garrett Juice plus garlic. See Rose Program in appendix.
- Fire Ants. Use Garden-Ville Fire Ant Control and beneficial nematodes.

ODD JOBS:
- Mow weekly and leave clippings on the lawn.
- Turn compost pile.
- Continue to add new vegetative matter and manure to existing and additional compost piles.
- Mulch all bare soil.
- Feed and water the birds!

*Planting recommendations based on North Texas climate. Check with your local nurseries and extension service for specific varieties and timing in your area.

MAY

PLANT:*
- Lawn grasses from plugs, sod, seed, or sprigs or by hydromulching. Also the tall prairie grasses from seed; big and little bluestem, Indiangrass, switchgrass, sideoats gramagrass, and eastern gamagrass.
- Tropical color in beds or pots: bougainvillea, mandevilla, allamanda, penta, hibiscus, and others.
- Trees and shrubs.
- Warm-season annual color plants: lantana, begonias, zinnia, periwinkle, cosmos, verbena, and others.
- Cannas, glads, caladiums, and other summer bulbs. Mums and other fall perennials.
- Ground covers from 1¼" or 4" pots. Hot-weather vegetables, including southern peas, okra, and melons.

FERTILIZE:
- All annual flowers and potted plants with organic fertilizers. Spray Garrett Juice on all foliage every two weeks.

PRUNE:
- Climbing roses, after their bloom.
- Spring-flowering shrubs, vines, and trees after they have bloomed.
- "Pinch" away the growing tips of mums weekly.

WATER:
- All planting areas deeply but infrequently during dry periods.
- Potted plants regularly. Add 1 ounce of Garrett Juice per gallon of water.

PEST CONTROL:
- Release trichogramma wasps for pecan casebearer and caterpillars.
- Fleas, ticks, and chiggers: natural diatomaceous earth in dry weather and beneficial nematodes anytime.
- Cabbage loopers and other caterpillars: *Bacillus thuringiensis* (Bt) or fire ant control formula.
- Aphids on tender, new growth: strong water blast and release ladybugs.
- Release green lacewings and ladybugs.
- Lacebugs on azaleas, sycamores: Spray garlic-pepper tea or Garden-Ville Fire Ant Control.
- Brown patch or other fungal diseases: apply cornmeal at 10–20 lbs./1,000 sq. ft.
- Weeds: Hand remove or use mechanical devices.

ODD JOBS:
- Mow weekly and leave clippings on the lawn.
- Turn compost pile and continue to add new ingredients.
- Mulch all bare soil.
- Feed and water the birds!

*Planting recommendations based on **North Texas climate**. Check with your local nurseries and extension service for specific varieties and timing in your area.*

JUNE

PLANT:*
- All warm-season grasses: bermuda, zoysia, St. Augustine, buffalo, and the tall prairie grasses.
- Summer annual color: portulaca, marigold, zinnia, periwinkle, lantana, copperleaf, amaranthus, cosmos, and verbena.
- Tropical color: bougainvillea, hibiscus, pentas, allamandas, mandevillas, etc.
- Shrubs and trees.
- Fall tomatoes.

FERTILIZE:
- All planting areas with organic fertilizer. This should be the second major fertilization. Use about 20 lbs./1,000 sq. ft.
- Spray all plantings and lawns with Garrett Juice every two weeks or at least once a month.
- Iron deficiency results in yellowed leaves with dark green veins on the youngest growth. Apply Texas greensand. Magnesium products will also help. Use high-calcium lime for calcium deficiency.

PRUNE:
- Blackberries, to remove fruiting canes after harvest. Prune new canes to 3' in height to encourage side branching.
- Remove spent flowers from daisies, daylilies, cannas, cornflowers, coreopsis, and other summer flowers.
- Dead and damaged wood from trees, shrubs, as needed.

WATER:
- All planting areas deeply but infrequently during dry periods.
- Potted plants regularly. Daily waterings are needed for some plants. Add an ounce per gallon of Garrett Juice at least once a month.

PEST CONTROL:
- Spider mites: Garrett Juice. Spray every three days for nine days.
- Fleas, ticks, chiggers: Dust with natural diatomaceous earth and release beneficial nematodes.
- Bagworms and other caterpillars: Release trichogramma wasps and spray if needed with (Bt) (*Bacillus thuringiensis*).
- Garrett Juice plus 2 ounces of orange oil per gallon of spray is also effective.
- Scale insects, including mealy bugs: Garden-Ville Fire Ant Control.
- Black spot on roses, mildew, and other fungi: Garrett Juice plus garlic tea or skim milk. See appendix for the Rose Program.
- Weeds: Hand remove and work on improving soil health.
- Lacebugs, elm leaf beetles: Spray garlic-pepper tea, summer-weight horticultural oil, or Garden-Ville Fire Ant Control.

ODD JOBS:
- Mow weekly and leave clippings on the lawn.
- Turn compost pile.
- Mulch all bare soil.
- Feed and water the birds!

Planting recommendations based on North Texas climate. Check with your local nurseries and extension service for specific varieties and timing in your area.

JULY

PLANT:*
- Color for fall: marigolds, zinnias, celosia, Joseph's coat, and asters.
- Container-grown nursery stock.
- Warm-seasonal lawn grasses.
- Tomatoes, peppers, melons, other warm-season vegetables for fall garden.
- Wildflower seed (better now than to wait until fall).

FERTILIZE:
- All planting areas with organic fertilizers, if not done in June.
- Use Texas greensand for iron deficiency. Use high calcium lime for calcium deficiency.
- Spray Garrett Juice on all foliage.

PRUNE:
- Roses, to encourage fall bloom.
- Dead or damaged limbs.
- Flowering plants, to remove spent flower heads and encourage new flower production.

WATER:
- All planting areas deeply but infrequently during dry periods.
- Outdoor container plants daily, others as needed.

PEST CONTROL:
- Chinch bugs: Dust natural diatomaceous earth or spray the fire ant control formula.
- Elm leaf beetles, lace bugs: Spray summer-weight horticultural oil, Garden-Ville Fire Ant Control, or *Bacillus thuringiensis* (Bt).
- Spider mites: Spray garlic-pepper tea or any spray that contains liquid seaweed.
- Fire ants: Drench with Garden-Ville Fire Ant Control. See appendix for formula.
- Fleas, ticks, chiggers, bermuda mites: Dust natural diatomaceous earth, and apply beneficial nematodes. Dust with sulfur in alkaline soils.
- Webworms and bagworms: *Bacillus thuringiensis* (Bt) with 1 teaspoon soap per gallon. Spray at dusk. Release trichogramma wasps.
- Leaf rollers: Spray *Bacillus thuringiensis* (Bt). Release trichogramma wasps.
- Scale insects on euonymus, hollies, camellias: Spray horticultural oil, or fire ant control formula or remove the unadapted plants.
- Weeds: Hand remove or use mechanical devices.

ODD JOBS:
- Mow weekly and leave clippings on the lawn.
- Turn compost pile, add new ingredients, and start new piles. Add molasses to piles to eliminate problems with fire ants.
- Mulch all bare soil with partially completed compost or other coarse-textured material.
- Feed and water the birds!

Planting recommendations based on North Texas climate. Check with your local nurseries and extension service for specific varieties and timing in your area.

AUGUST

PLANT:*
- Fall color such as mums, asters, marigolds, zinnias, and celosia.
- Fall-flowering bulbs such as spider lilies, fall crocus, and fall amaryllis.
- Finish fall vegetable plantings of beans, corn, cucumbers, melons, and squash.
- Cool-season vegetables, including broccoli, cauliflower, brussels sprouts, cabbage, spinach, potatoes, lettuce, carrots, beets, radishes, and English peas.
- Finish planting warm-season lawn grasses: buffalo, bermuda, St. Augustine, and zoysia.
- Wildflower seed if you haven't already.

FERTILIZE:
- Foliar-feed all planting beds and lawns with Garrett Juice every two weeks.

PRUNE:
- Trim spent flower stalks and blossoms of annuals and perennials to stimulate regrowth and more blooms.
- Remove dead and damaged wood from shrubs and trees.

WATER:
- Water deeply and as infrequently as possible. Your garden and landscape will usually need more water this month than any other.
- Potted plants and hanging baskets daily or as needed.

PEST CONTROL:
- Grubworms: Good soil culture is the best control. Apply beneficial nematodes as needed.
- Chinch bugs: Dust natural diatomaceous earth or spray the Garden-Ville Fire Ant Control.
- Aphids: Garrett Juice and garlic tea. Water blast and release of ladybugs. Add molasses at 2 oz./gallon of spray.
- Fire Ants: Garden-Ville Fire Ant Control for large areas. Soapy water or diatomaceous earth for individual mounds. Apply beneficial nematodes. Broadcast orange or grapefruit peelings pulp.
- Chewing insects: Broadcast beneficial nematodes. Dust natural diatomaceous earth or spray Garrett Juice plus garlic. Add 2 ounces per gallon orange oil for the hard to control insects.
- Cabbage loopers and other caterpillars: Release trichogramma wasps and spray *Bacillus thuringiensis* (Bt).
- Borers in peaches, plums, and other fruit trees: Use the Organic Fruit and Pecan Tree Program. See the appendix.
- Release beneficial insects if needed: praying mantids, ladybugs, green lacewings, etc.

ODD JOBS:
- Mow weekly and leave clippings on the lawn.
- Turn compost pile.
- Feed and water the birds!

*Planting recommendations based on North Texas climate. Check with your local nurseries and extension service for specific varieties and timing in your area.

SEPTEMBER

PLANT:*
- Cool-season, leafy root crops such as carrots, beets, turnips, etc.
- Wildflower seeds, if you haven't already.
- Finish warm-season lawn grass plantings by early September.
- Transplant established spring-flowering bulbs, iris, daylilies, daisies, and peonies.
- Perennials.
- Cool-season grasses.

FERTILIZE:
- All planting areas with organic fertilizer at approximately 10–20 lbs./1,000 sq. ft.
- Foliar feed all planting areas and lawns with Garrett Juice.

PRUNE:
- Root-prune wisterias that failed to bloom.
- Remove spent blooms of summer flowering perennials.
- Remove surface tree roots if needed, but no more than 20 percent of root system per year.

WATER:
- Water deeply during dry spells.
- Potted plants and hanging baskets regularly. Add 1 ounce of Garrett Juice per gallon of water at least twice.

PEST CONTROL:
- Brown patch in St. Augustine: Garrett Juice plus garlic or skim milk. Apply cornmeal at 10–20 lbs./1,000 sq. ft.
- Webworms, tent caterpillars: *Bacillus thuringiensis* (Bt).
- Grubworms: beneficial nematodes.
- Cabbage loopers on broccoli, cauliflower, cabbage, brussels sprouts: Spray *Bacillus thuringiensis* (Bt) and release trichogramma wasps.
- Aphids on tender, new fall growth: Garlic tea or water blast followed by release of ladybugs. Add 1–2 ounces of molasses per gallon of spray.
- Fire ants: Drench mounds with Garden-Ville Fire Ant Control and release beneficial nematodes.
- Roses for black spot and powdery mildew: See the Organic Rose Program in appendix.
- Iron chlorosis (yellowed leaves, dark green veins, newest growth first): chelated iron, and sulfur. Epsom salts or Sul-Po-Mag if magnesium is deficient. Texas greensand is the best treatment.

ODD JOBS:
- Mow weekly and leave clippings on the lawn.
- Turn the compost pile.
- Feed and water the birds!

Planting recommendations based on North Texas climate. Check with your local nurseries and extension service for specific varieties and timing in your area.

OCTOBER

PLANT:*

- Pansies, violas, pinks, snapdragons, flowering cabbage and kale, garlic, English daisies, Iceland poppies, wallflowers, and other cool-season flowers.
- Complete wildflower plantings.
- Trees, shrubs, vines, and spring- and summer-flowering perennials.
- Strawberries.
- Cool-season grasses.

FERTILIZE:

- Foliar-feed all plantings and lawns with Garrett Juice. Mulch all bare soil. Add new material to the top of all existing mulch where bare soil is exposed.

WATER:

- Newly planted wildflower areas if no rain.
- Newly planted annuals.

PRUNE:

- Pick-prune shrubs as needed, begin major tree pruning for winter.
- Remove dead and damaged wood from trees.

PESTS:

- Brown patch in St. Augustine: Broadcast cornmeal at 10–20 lbs./1,000 sq. ft.
- Peach leaf curl: See the Fruit and Pecan Program in the appendix.
- Cabbage loopers in garden: Spray *Bacillus thuringiensis* (Bt) and release trichogramma wasps.
- To reflower a poinsettia, give it uninterrupted darkness 14 hours each day and 10 hours of bright light each day until December. It's better to buy new plants each year.

ODD JOBS:

- Mulch all bare soil.
- Mow weekly and leave the clippings on the lawn.
- Build new compost piles and turn old ones.
- Use completed compost to prepare new planting beds.
- Use partially completed compost as a topdressing mulch for ornamentals and vegetables.
- Feed and water the birds!

*Planting recommendations based on North Texas climate. Check with your local nurseries and extension service for specific varieties and timing in you area.

NOVEMBER

PLANT:*
- Trees and shrubs.
- Spring bulbs, including daffodils and grape hyacinths. Precool tulips and Dutch hyacinths for 45 days at 40° prior to planting.
- Spring- and summer-flowering perennials, including daisies, iris, daylilies, lilies, thrift, lythrum, etc.
- Finish planting spring-flowering annuals, including pansies, pinks, snapdragons, flowering cabbage and kale, English daisies, California and Iceland poppies.
- Winter-hardy nursery stock.
- Cool-season grasses.

FERTILIZE:
- Bulbs, annuals, and perennials with earthworm castings and other gentle, organic fertilizers.
- Indoor plants with earthworm castings, lava sand, and other low-odor, organic fertilizers.

WATER:
- All planting areas at least once if no rain.

PRUNE:
- Begin major tree pruning. Remove dead limbs before leaves fall.
- Pick-prune shrubs to remove longest shoots if needed.
- Remove spent blooms and seed heads from flowering plants.
- Cut off tops of brown perennials. Leave roots in the soil.

PESTS:
- Watch roots of removed annuals for nematodes (knots on the roots). Treat infected soil with biostimulants, molasses, compost, and citrus pulp.
- Watch houseplants for spider mites, scale, aphids. Spray as needed with biostimulants and mild soap and seaweed. Use lightweight oils as a last resort.
- Watch lawn for signs of grubworm damage. Grass will be loose on top of ground. Treat with beneficial nematodes.

ODD JOBS:
- Have landscape and garden soils tested now to determine soil-balancing needs.
- Pick tomatoes the night before the first freeze. Let them ripen indoors.
- Put all fallen leaves, spent annuals, and other vegetative matter into the compost piles.
- Add mulch to your garden. Do not cultivate once healthy soil has been developed.
- Mulch all bare ornamental beds for winter protection.
- Turn compost piles.
- Feed and water the birds!

Planting recommendations based on North Texas climate. Check with your local nurseries and extension service for specific varieties and timing in your area.

DECEMBER

PLANT:*
- Trees and shrubs
- Living Christmas trees (after use) that are adapted to the area's climate and soils.
- Spring bulbs, including tulips and hyacinths.

FERTILIZE:
- Greenhouse plants, if needed, with organic fertilizers, earthworm castings, and lava sand.
- Houseplants, once or twice during winter, with earthworm castings, lava sand, other odorless organic fertilizers. Add 1 tbs./gallon natural apple cider vinegar.

WATER:
- Any dry areas to help protect against winter cold injury.

PRUNE:
- Evergreens to adjust the appearance.
- Shade trees to remove dead and damaged wood.
- Cut off tops of spent perennials. Leave roots in the ground.

PESTS:
- Bark aphids on trees: No treatment needed.
- Scale insects on shade and fruit trees: horticultural oil for heavy infestation.
- Cut mistletoe out of trees. Remove infested limbs if possible.
- Spray houseplants with seaweed, mild soap, and biostimulants to control scale, mealy bugs, spider mites, and other insects. Add vinegar to the irrigation water.
- Remember that henbit, clover, and other wildflowers are beautiful, so don't worry about spraying them.

ODD JOBS:
- Pick tomatoes the night before first freeze.
- Clean and oil tools before storing for winter.
- Run mower, trimmer engines dry of gasoline. Drain and change oil. Take to repair shop now to avoid the spring rush.
- Mulch all bare soil.
- Turn compost piles.
- Feed and water the birds!

GENERAL:
- Vinegar isn't needed in the irrigation if the water is acid in pH.

*Planting recommendations based on North Texas climate. Check with your local nurseries and extension service for specific varieties and timing in your area.

PEST CONTROL 6

"The answer to pest problems is not in a bag of poisonous chemicals, but in a better understanding of the laws of Nature and a desire to work with these laws."

Malcolm Beck, San Antonio 1988

Ever wondered how insects were kept under control or why plants weren't devoured by destructive insects before man started to "control" the environment? The answer lies in the fact that Nature has a balanced, natural order.

With the proliferation of chemicals during the twentieth century, many beneficial insects have been killed along with the harmful insects. Generally, the harmful ones will reestablish themselves more quickly than will the beneficial ones, and plant loss accelerates. Encouraging the beneficial insects to be established again is a primary goal of an organic program. However, there are many safe or low-toxic products available to transition from a chemical program to an organic program that will reduce the harmful effects to beneficial insect populations.

A report by the scientific journal *Bioscience* says that a mere 1 percent of the pesticides applied to plants ever reaches its ultimate destination—the pest insects. The other 99 percent pollute and poison the air, soil, water, good bugs, animals, and man.

This section is divided into two parts—one on harmful insects and one on beneficial insects. We will first discuss the beneficial insects and how they can help keep the harmful insects under control. After all, keeping them under control is all that is really needed, since the ones that are not killed will serve as a lure for the beneficial insects. We will then discuss the major harmful insects, along with how to control them, primarily with biological and/or botanical pesticides.

BENEFICIAL INSECTS

It would be impossible to cover all the beneficial insects because somewhere around 98 percent of the world's insects are beneficial. It could be argued that even the destructive bugs are good because they eliminate weak plants.

The best way to control troublesome insects is to allow them to control themselves. Nature provides beautiful checks and balances if we allow them to function. Friendly bugs are being used more and more to help control destructive insects in vegetable gardens, stored grain, greenhouses, and orchards. Parasitic mites and wasps are being used to control houseflies, barnyard flies, and fire ants. Earthworms, centipedes, and millipedes are not technically insects, but they are beneficial, especially earthworms. Centipedes and millipedes are helpful because they aerate the soil, produce nutrients, and help break down organic material.

A critical element of an organic program is the establishment and maintenance of biodiversity. That means the vegetable garden and landscaping need to have a healthy and dynamic mix of insects, plants, animals, and birds. Man needs to fit into that puzzle as well. Here's some information on the insects and other critters that can help you maintain your gardens.

See *Texas Bug Book* by Malcom Beck and Howard Garrett for additional information on using beneficial insects and controlling insect pests.

BENEFICIAL INSECTS
GROUND BEETLES

One-third of all animals and 40 percent of all insects are beetles. All beetles have hard, opaque wing covers that meet in a straight line down the middle of their backs. The ground beetles are important predators of plant-eating insects. They usually feed at night on soft-bodied larvae such as cankerworms, tent caterpillars, slugs, and snails. Soldier beetles feed on aphids, grasshopper eggs, cucumber beetles, and various caterpillars.

LADYBUGS

larva

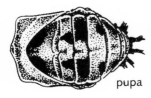

pupa

adult

Ladybird beetle is the proper term, but these little friends are best known as ladybugs. The ladybug is the most popular and most universally known beneficial insect. There are several hundred different kinds in North America and all are beneficial. They are all very helpful and should be protected. The convergent ladybug (orange with black spots) is the most available commercially.

Yellow ladybug eggs are visible in the winter and early spring in clusters on the backs of leaves and on the trunks of trees. The adult ladybug can eat 200 aphids per day, the larvae 70–100 per day. The larvae and the adult beetles eat large quantities of aphids and other small, soft-bodied insects such as scale, thrips, and mealy bugs. They should be released after aphids are visible and at night after the foliage has been sprinkled with water. Let a few out at a time to see if they are hungry. If they fly away, put them in the refrigerator for a day or two and try again later after they have used up their stored food. Ladybugs will store in the refrigerator for a few days (35–45° is best for storage). They will remain dormant and alive under these cool temperatures, although storage tends to dry them out and a few will die. They will naturalize if chemical sprays are eliminated.

For ladybugs to mature and lay eggs, they need a nectar and pollen source, such as flowering plants. Legumes such as peas, beans, clover, and alfalfa are especially good. To make an artificial food, dilute a little honey with a small amount of water and mix in a little brewer's yeast or bee pollen. Streak tiny amounts of this mixture on small pieces of waxed paper, and fasten these to plants. Replace these every 5–6 days, or when they become moldy. Keep any extra food refrigerated between feedings. The ladybug's favorite real food is the aphid.

If ladybugs are released indoors or in a greenhouse, you might want to screen off any openings to prevent their escape.

FIREFLIES (LIGHTNING BUGS)

The firefly is a fascinating insect that produces a light by releasing luciferin from its abdomen to combine with oxygen. When conditions are right the male flashes his light every six seconds to be answered by the female two seconds later. Firefly larvae feed on snails, slugs, cutworms, and mites.

GREEN LACEWINGS

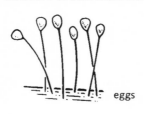

eggs

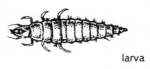

larva

cocoon

adult

The green lacewing is a beautiful, fragile, light-green or brown insect with lustrous, yellow eyes. The adult is approximately ½" long, holds its wings up tent-like when at rest, and feeds on honeydew, nectar, and pollen. The adults really aren't terribly beneficial. They just fly around, look pretty, and mate. The larvae, on the other hand, are voracious eaters of aphids, red spider mites, thrips, mealybugs, cottony cushion scale, and many worms.

The lacewing larvae (also known as "aphid lions") emerge from the eggs that appear on the end of thin white filaments attached to leaves or stems. The larvae pupates by spinning a cocoon with silken thread. The adult emerges in about five days by cutting a hole in the cocoon.

If it is inconvenient to release the lacewing immediately after purchase, the eggs or larvae may be refrigerated for a few days, but be careful not to freeze. A temperature of 38° to 45°F will delay development but not hurt the eggs.

Eggs and larvae can be hand sprinkled wherever harmful insects exist or are suspected. Even if you put them in the wrong place, they will search almost 100 feet for their first meal. One of the best ways to distribute lacewing eggs and larvae is with a pill bottle with a small hole in the cap. A salt shaker will work but you have to increase the size of the holes. A thimble will hold about 10,000 eggs. Releasing the green lacewing from a card or cup mounted in a tree will keep the fire ants from getting them before they do their work. It helps to put a sticky material such as Tanglefoot on the trunk of the tree to block the ants' access. Apply it to paper wrapped around the trunk to prevent girdling.

Lacewing larvae are gray in color. They look like tiny alligators and mature in 2–3 weeks. Biweekly releases are ideal. Flowering plants attract green lacewings; buckwheat is especially good.

PREDATORY MITES

The adult predatory mite is orange in color. The immature stages are a pale salmon color. They can be differentiated from the "red" two-spotted spider mite by the lack of spots on either side. The body is pear-shaped, and the front legs are longer than those of pest mites. Predatory mites move about quickly when disturbed or exposed to bright light, and they multiply twice as quickly as pest mites do, with the females laying about 50 eggs. They eat from 5 to 20 eggs or mites per day.

Release predatory mites at the first sign of spider mite damage. For heavy infestations, you will probably need to reduce the populations of pest mites with organic sprays such as Garrett Juice plus orange oil at 2 ounces per gallon of spray.

PRAYING MANTISES

These fierce-looking but friendly critters will eat almost any insect, especially caterpillars, grasshoppers, beetles, and other damaging pests. Be careful not to confuse the egg cases with the asp or puss caterpillar, which is a soft, hairy insect with a powerful sting. The praying mantis egg case looks very similar but is hard like papier-maché. The only negative about praying mantises is that they also eat beneficial insects. They don't usually eat ladybugs, however, because ladybugs are bitter.

SPIDERS

Most spiders are beneficial and harmless with the exceptions of the black widow and brown recluse. Brown recluse spiders have become more common the last few years. They are normally found indoors. You'll rarely see a brown recluse because they seek out dark corners in closets, etc., and move about at night. The female black widow is easy to identify by the red hourglass on her abdomen. Beware of her because her venomous sting is very powerful and can cause illness and even death. The puny little male isn't much trouble; in fact, the female devours him after mating.

WASPS

All wasps and mud daubers are beneficial. One of their favorite foods is the tent caterpillar that often disfigures pecan trees. The tiny trichogramma wasp is very effective for controlling cutworms, moths, and the pecan casebearer by laying its eggs on the eggs of the pests. When the wasp's eggs hatch, the larvae feed on the eggs of the pest. Wasps will sting only if you threaten them, and the mud dauber only if you grab it! So don't! Trichogramma and other friendly wasps don't sting at all. The mud dauber's favorite food is the black widow spider. It's also good for controlling flies in horse stables. Braconid wasps kill pests by laying their eggs in hosts like hornworms, codling moths, and aphids.

TRICHOGRAMMA WASPS

Trichogramma wasps or "moth egg parasites" are used to control pecan casebearer, cabbage worms, tomato hornworms, corn earworms, and other caterpillars. They are almost microscopic parasitic wasps which attack over 200 types of worm pests. The trichogramma wasp stings the pest worm egg and deposits its own egg inside. The egg hatches and the larva feeds on and kills the pest.

Early application of trichogramma before a problem has been diagnosed is the ideal way to begin a pest control program. Weekly or biweekly releases throughout the early growing season are ideal.

WHITEFLY PARASITES

The whitefly parasite can help to deter serious damage to tomatoes, cucumbers, and ornamental plants. *Encarsia formosa* is a small, efficient parasite of the whitefly. It is about the size of a spider mite. It attacks the whitefly in the immature stages, laying eggs in the third and fourth stages, while feeding off the first and second stages. Early application of *Encarsia formosa* prior to heavy infestations is recommended. Parasites should be released at the first sign of whitefly.

NEMATODES

Beneficial nematodes are microscopic round-worms used to control cutworms, armyworms, corn rootworms, cabbage loopers, Colorado potato beetles, grubworms, termites, fleas, fire ants, and other soil pests. Nematodes enter the insect pest through the mouth or other body openings. Once inside the host, the nematodes feed and reproduce until the food supply is gone. Then hordes of nematodes emerge in search of new victims. Sounds pretty gross, doesn't it? Early applications prior to heavy pest infestations, followed by monthly applications, are the ideal solution.

Heterorhabditis (Heteros) are best for grubs. Steinernema (Steiners) work for grubs but are better for moths. Other beneficial insects include syrphid flies, parasitodes, big-eyed bugs, pirate bugs, and many, many others. For more details on beneficial insects see the *Texas Bug Book*.

> And, of course, anyplace you use beneficial insects, you'll want to avoid spraying with pesticides.

SOURCES FOR BENEFICIAL BUGS*

A-1 Unique Insect Control - 5504 Sperry Drive, Citrus Heights, CA 95621, (916) 961–7945, Fax (916) 967–7082,
Website: www.a-1unique.com E-mail: ladybugs.@a-1unique.com

American Insectaries, Inc. - 30805 Rodrigues Road, Escondido, CA 92026, (760) 751–1436, Fax (760) 749–7061

Arbico - P.O. Box 4247, Tucson, AZ 85738, (800) 827–2847
Beneficial Insect Co. - 244 Forest Street, Fort Mill, SC 29715, (803) 547–2301

Beneficial Insectary - 14751 Oak Run Road, Oak Run, CA 96069, (530) 472–3715

BioAg Supply - 710 South Columbia, Plainview, TX 79072
(806) 293-5861, 1-800-746-9900 Fax (806) 293-0712

BioCrop Care - P.O. Box 87, Mathis, TX 78368
1-800-233-4914 info@biofac.com

BioLogic - Springtown Road, P.O. Box 177, Willow Hill, PA 17271
(717) 349–2789

Buena Biosystems - P.O. Box 4008, Ventura, CA 93007, (805) 525–2525
Gulf Coast Biotic Technology - 72 West Oaks, Huntsville, TX 77340
(800) 524–1958

Hydro-Gardens, Inc. - P.O. Box 25845, Colorado Springs, CO 80936
(800) 634–6362

Kunafin Trichogramma Industries - Route 1, Box 39
Quemado, TX 78877, (800) 832–1113, Fax (830) 757–1468

M&R Durango - P.O. Box 886, Bayfield, CO 81122, (800) 526–4075

New Earth, Inc. - 9810 Taylorsville Rd., Louisville, KY 40299
(502) 261–0005

N-VIRO Products, Ltd. - 610 Walnut Ave., Bohemia, NY 11716
(516) 567–2628

OrCon, Inc. - 5132 Venice Blvd., Los Angeles, CA 90019, 213-937-7444.

Organic Pest Management - P.O. Box 55267, Seattle, WA 98155,
206-367-0707.

Oxnard Pest Control Association - 632 Pacific Ave., P.O. Box 1187
Oxnard, CA 93032, (805)483–1024, Fax (805) 487–6867

Peaceful Valley Farm Supply - P.O. Box 2209, Grass Valley, CA 95945
(916) 272–4769

Planet Natural - P.O. Box 3146, Bozeman, MT 59772, (406) 587–5891
(800) 289–6656

Rincon-Vitova Insectaries, Inc. - P.O. Box 1555, Ventura, CA 93022
(805) 643–5407, (800) 248–2847

The Beneficial Insect Co. - 244 Forest Street, Fort Mill, SC 29715
(803) 547–2301

Tri-Cal Biosystems - P.O. Box 1327, Hollister, CA 95024
(408) 637–0195

Worm's Way, Inc. - 3151 South Highway 446, Bloomington, IN 47401
 (800) 274–9676

HARMFUL INSECTS
APHIDS

Aphids are sucking insects that can destroy the tender growth of plants, causing stunted and curled leaf growth and leaving a honeydew deposit. They can be controlled by strong blasts of water and the release of ladybugs. Protecting ladybugs and lacewings and promoting soil health and biodiversity is the best control for these indicator pests. Regular releases of beneficial insects give excellent control, but adapted plants and healthy soil is the best permanent control.

ANTS

There are many different ants, including carpenter ants, fire ants, and pharaoh ants. Solutions for ants indoors include natural diatomaceous earth, boric acid, cinnamon, and baking soda. Outdoors, treat fire ant mounds with Garden-Ville Soil Conditioner. Treat the site with beneficial nematodes and go organic. The competition of microorganisms, insects, lizards, frogs, toads, birds, and even plants is not enjoyed by fire ants. Control carpenter and other house ants with sweet baits that contain small amounts of boric acid. Citrus oil sprays will also kill them.

BAGWORMS

Bagworms are a common pest of ornamental trees and some shrubs. They will prey on many different species of plants such as cedar, juniper, cypress, etc. In the larval stage they can defoliate trees. They can be controlled with *Bacillus thuringiensis* (Bt) in the spring. Hand picking the bags is also beneficial for control. Trichogramma wasps can help to control problem infestations.

BEES

Bees are beneficial and should be protected. For the proper environmental control, contact the beekeeper club or society in your area. They will usually come and get them or give you advice on control. But if you must kill problem bees, use soapy water. Toxic poisons should never be used, especially to kill out colonies. Other bees forage the poisoned honey late in the season and kill out their own colonies. Our pollinator populations are seriously on the decline because of the use of toxic chemical pesticides.

BEETLES

Many adult beetles eat plant foliage and can destroy plants completely. An effective solution for destructive beetles is dry natural diatomaceous earth and a spray of Garrett Juice plus orange oil at 2 ounces/gallon of spray. Garlic tea is an even less toxic control. It's important to remember that many beetles are beneficial and only eat problem insects.

BORERS

Borers attack sick softwood trees and various trees in stress. Adult beetles will eat tender terminal growth and then deposit their eggs in the base of the tree. Eggs hatch into larvae and bore into trees and tunnel through the wood until the tree is weakened. Active, tunneling larvae can be killed with a stiff wire run into the holes. Beneficial nematodes applied directly in holes will usually kill active larvae, but keeping trees healthy and out of stress is the best prevention. A generous amount of diatomaceous earth at the base of susceptible trees will also help. Applying beneficial nematodes to the soil is also effective. Tree Trunk Goop (see appendix) is also helpful.

CABBAGE LOOPERS

Cabbage loopers are the larvae of those moths that are brown with silver spots in the middle of each wing. They can be killed with Bt (*Bacillus thuringiensis*) spray when the insects are young. Use soap as a surfactant and spray late in the day since these guys feed at night. Trichogramma wasps will also help control these critters. It's interesting that even the chemical "pushers" admit that the chemical insecticides are ineffective at controlling loopers.

CANKERWORMS

The cankerworm hangs on a silk thread from trees. He or she doesn't do a lot of damage. Wasps will usually control them. If not, use Bt (*Bacillus thuringiensis*) or fire ant control for heavy infestations.

CATERPILLARS

Caterpillars are best known for their ability to defoliate trees and veggies. *Bacillus thuringiensis* (Bt) is an excellent biological control. Wasps are also a great help in controlling caterpillars of all kinds. Remember that caterpillars grow up to be beautiful butterflies, so don't kill them all.

CHIGGERS

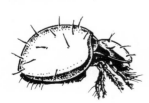

Chiggers are known for their very annoying bite. The itching usually starts the day after you are bitten and lasts two to four days. Natural diatomaceous earth and sulfur will help prevent bites and control the critters. Vinegar rubbed on bites will eliminate the itching.

CHINCH BUGS

Chinch bugs are tiny, black and white, pin-head-size or smaller bugs. During hot, dry weather, chinch bugs can destroy unhealthy lawns. The lawns will look yellow, turn brown, and then die. A dusting of natural diatomaceous earth works in the hot dry weather, also Garrett Juice plus orange oil. This insect hardly ever attacks healthy, well-maintained grass.

CRICKETS

Crickets live in and out of doors, destroy fabrics such as wool, cotton, synthetics, and silk, and also attack plants. Their irritating sound is the primary objection, although they will eat tender sprouts of wildflowers and vegetables. Solutions outdoors include natural diatomaceous earth, and boric acid for indoor use. *Nosema locustae* is a biological bait for overall control. Citrus oil sprays will also kill them.

ELM LEAF BEETLES

Wherever there is an American, Siberian, or cedar elm tree, the elm leaf beetle can be found. The elm leaf beetle will eat and damage foliage and then move to the next tree. Trees can die from defoliation but only unhealthy trees are seriously attacked by elm leaf beetles. Solutions include Garden-Ville Fire Ant Control and *Bacillus thuringiensis* (Bt). Strong populations of beneficial insects will also help.

FIRE ANTS

Spray the infested site with Garden-Ville Fire Ant Control formula (same as Garden-Ville Soil Conditioner) or any citrus oil, compost tea, and molasses mix. Drench mounds with Garden-Ville Fire Ant Control formula (citrus oil, molasses, and compost tea).

Treat the site with beneficial nematodes. These are living organisms and must be used before the date deadline on the package.

Go organic. The biodiversity of microbes, insects, and other animals is the best long-term control. Spray the site regularly with Garrett Juice.

Homemade Garden-Ville Fire Ant Control: Mix one part compost tea, one part molasses, and one part citrus oil concentrate. Mix at 4–6 ounces per gallon of water for treating fire ant mounds. Grapefruit and orange peeling ground into a pulp can be put on fire ant mounds to help with the control.

3-Step Fire Ant Program

1. Drench mounds with orange oil products.
2. Release beneficial nematodes.
3. Go organic.

FLEAS AND TICKS

Spray the infested site with Garden-Ville Fire Ant Control formula (same as Garden-Ville Soil Conditioner) or any citrus oil, compost tea, and molasses mix.

Treat the site with beneficial nematodes. These are living organisms so use before the date deadline on the package.

Dust pet sleeping quarters, if necessary, with natural diatomaceous earth.

Bathe pets with herbal shampoos. The most effective products contain citrus (d-limonene) and tea tree oil (melaleuca). Citrus may burn cats' skin.

Spray the site regularly with Garrett Juice.

Homemade Garden-Ville Fire Ant Control: Mix one part compost tea, one part molasses, and one part citrus oil concentrate. Mix at 4–6 ounces per gallon of water for treating fire ant mounds.

FLIES

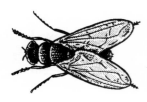

Flies can be repelled with fresh, crushed tansy or garlic. They can also be killed with fly swatters. On the farm they can be greatly reduced by feeding the animals natural diatomaceous earth daily at 2 percent of their ratios. Fly parasites are the most economical and most effective control.

FLEA HOPPERS

This is a common vegetable-garden pest. It sucks juices from the foliage and causes a loss of leaf color which stresses plants. Sulfur and natural diatomaceous earth will help.

FOREST TENT CATERPILLARS

These caterpillars will sometimes do some damage in early spring, but if pesticides are avoided, the beneficial wasps will usually keep these guys under control. Bt (*Bacillus thuringiensis*) can be used if they get out of hand. At worst they are only a temporary problem. They can also be killed with the fire ant control mix. Release Trichogramma wasps.

FUNGUS GNATS

Fungus gnats are present when the soil surface is too wet. They do little, if any, damage but are annoying. They can be gotten rid of by drying out the soil. Baking soda sprayed lightly on soil will quickly solve the problem. A Neem drench is also effective. Citrus oil spray kills them on contact.

GRASSHOPPERS

Spray Garrett Juice mixed with 2 ounces of citrus oil per gallon. Add 1 qt. of kaoline clay per 2 gallons of water with 1 tablespoon liqid soap. Adding garlic/pepper tea to the mix also helps. Dust the plants with all-purpose flour which forms a glue as the insects try to feed. Go organic. Plant a strongly biodiverse garden and landscape. In other words, use lots of different plants and yes, encourage the various insect eating animals. A biological bait, *Nosema locustae*, is also available and helpful with the overall program. When the humidity is low, dust plants with natural diatomaceous earth. Cover bare soil with mulch and feed the birds regularly.

GRUBWORMS

Grubworms are the larvae of June bugs. The adult beetles will chew some leaves and the grubs will eat the roots of grass and garden plants. Not all grubs are harmful; in fact, only about 10 percent of the species eat plant roots. The other 90 percent eat decaying organic matter, aerate the soil, and are beneficial. Control of the bad guys comes from being organic and having healthy soil with lots of beneficial organisms and other insects. To speed up the control, apply beneficial nematodes and small amounts of sugar or molasses.

LACEBUGS

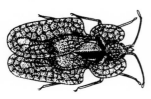

Lacebugs attack various deciduous trees and broad-leafed evergreens. The lacebug is flat and oval and sucks the sap from the underside of the leaf. A quick solution for this pest is garlic/pepper tea and natural diatomaceous earth. Healthy biodiversity in the garden will eliminate a destructive population of this pest. Garrett Juice plus orange oil will also help.

LEAFHOPPERS

Leafhoppers excrete honeydew and damage leaves by stripping them, causing stunted, dwarfed, and yellow foliage. They can be controlled with a mix of Garrett Juice and garlic tea or simply by the encouragement of diverse populations of beneficial insects.

LEAF MINERS

Leaf miners will cause brown foliage tips which often continue over the entire leaf. Neem products are effective. Garrett Juice/garlic tea spray will help. They cause minor damage only, so treatment is rarely needed.

LEAF SKELETONIZERS

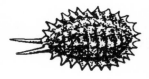

These insects are sawflies. They do cosmetic damage to red oak and other tree leaves. It's rarely necessary to treat. Damage is usually confined to isolated spots in the foliage.

MEALYBUGS

Mealybugs are sucking insects that look like cotton on plant stems. Mealybugs suck sap from the foliage and stems and can destroy plants. Mealybugs like warm weather and also infest houseplants. Helpful controls include soap and water, predator insects, natural diatomaceous earth, and lizards. For houseplant problems, dab alcohol on bugs with a cotton swab.

MOSQUITOES

Mosquitoes are easier to control with organic techniques than with toxic chemicals. Here's the plan.

Empty standing water where possible. Treat water that cannot be emptied with gambusia fish or Bti (*Bacillus thuringiensis* 'Israelensis') product such as Bactimos Briquettes.

Spray for adult mosquitoes with garlic/pepper tea or Garden-Ville Fire Ant Control formula (see below). Citronella sprays are also effective.

Use organic management to encourage birds, bats, dragonflies, and other beneficial insects.

Use skin repellents that contain natural herbs such as aloe vera, citronella, eucalyptus, tea tree, and citrus oil.

Bug light devices do not work! Not unless you chain your dog to the device to provide the carbon dioxide! Mosquitoes are attracted to living organisms, not cold machines.

Garden-Ville Fire Ant Control formula: One part compost tea, one part molasses, one part citrus oil. Use four ounces of concentrate per gallon of spray. There are two ready-to-use commercial products that contain this mixture: Garden-Ville Fire Ant Control and GreenSense Soil Drench.

NEMATODES

Many nematodes are beneficial, but there are those that will attack ornamental trees, garden plants, and lawn grass. Controls include increasing the organic level in soil, using organic fertilizers, and applying products that increase microbial activity. Cedar flakes applied to the soil surface will also help. Citrus pulp tilled into the soil prior to planting also helps greatly.

PILL BUGS

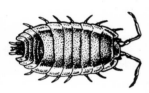

Pill bugs, or sow bugs, or roly-poly bugs are crustaceans and related to shrimp, crabs, and crawfish. They are found in damp places and feed on organic matter but when abundant will also eat plants. Beer in a trap is still one solution. Banana peels attract them so you can scoop them up and drop into a soapy water solution. A mix of cedar flakes, hot pepper, and natural diatomaceous earth is effective. Mulch using shredded cedar.

PLUM CURCULIOS

See the Fruit and Pecan Program in the appendix. It's a waste of time but you can do it if you want to attack this pest. Thick mulch, at least 4" of compost, rough bark, or tree chips is important. Regular spraying of garlic tea is one of the best organic preventatives. Biodiversity is critical for control of this pest. Spray foliage biweekly with Garrett Juice plus garlic tea.

RED SPIDER MITES

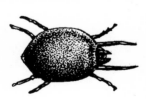

Red spider mites are very small and feed on garden plants and ornamental trees. You probably will not see the mites but you will notice the webbing that accompanies them. The best control is beneficial insects such as green lacewings. Controls also include spraying Garrett Juice plus garlic and extra seaweed. Strong blasts of water or soapy water are good for small infestations. Predatory mites are also effective.

ROACHES

There are numerous cockroaches, but only a few really pose a problem. Cockroaches usually live outdoors and are nocturnal by nature. Roaches will enter a home or building through any crack or crevice. Roaches will chew on cloth or books. Some solutions are the vigorous application of a shoe, rolled-up newspaper, natural diatomaceous earth, keeping your house clean, eliminating drips, leaks, and standing water, and sealing all openings. A light dusting of boric acid or natural diatomaceous earth indoors gives effective control. Spray with citrus products. See the appendix for bait formulas.

SCALE

Scale insects attach to stems, branches, and trunks and suck sap from the plants. Controls include horticultural oil, and Garden-Ville Fire Ant Control. Use soap and water with seaweed on interior plants. The black, scale-eating ladybug feeds on scale insects outdoors.

SLUGS

Slugs and snails must be kept moist at all times and will go anywhere there is moisture. Effective controls include garlic/pepper tea and natural diatomaceous earth, beer traps, and wood ashes. They can also be repelled with a mix of natural diatomaceous earth, hot pepper, and cedar flakes.

SQUASH BUGS

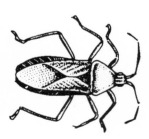

Squash bugs are difficult-to-control bugs that attack squash, cucumbers, pumpkins, and other cucurbits. Control by smashing the eggs, dusting the adults with natural diatomaceous earth, and planting lemon balm in between plants. Dusting young plants regularly with cheap self-rising flour will also help. Treat soil with beneficial nematodes and spray with Garrett Juice plus citrus oil. Planting a larger number of plants also seems to help.

SQUASH VINE BORERS

The squash vine borer is an insect whose larva is a worm that bores into the base stem of squash, cucumber, melon, gourd, and pumpkin. Controls: Cut the stem open, remove the worms, and cover the wounded area with soil. Another way is to inject Bt (*Bacillus thuringiensis*) into the base of the stem with a syringe. Spraying with Bt will also help. Treat soil with beneficial nematodes.

STINK BUGS

Stink bugs sting fruit and cause rotted spots. Some stink bugs are beneficial. They can be controlled with a spray of Garrett Juice plus citrus oil.

TERMITES

Treat all exposed wood with boric acid products such as Tim-Bor or Bora-Care. Inject these same products by foam into the walls. Use 00 sandblasting sand (also sold as 16 grit sand) as a physical barrier in leave-outs in slabs, against the edge of slabs, and on both sides of beams. New construction can use it under slabs. Treat the soil around the structure with beneficial nematodes. Ignore the nuts that say to remove the mulch from around the house. There is a new product call Bio-Blast which is a beneficial fungus product.

THRIPS

Thrips attack the buds and tight-petaled flowers such as roses, mums, and peonies. Thrips are not visible to the naked eye but will rasp the plant tissue and drain the sap. When there is a heavy infestation, they can kill a plant. Thrips are general eaters and will attack flowers or field crops. Controls include spraying Garrett Juice plus garlic and releasing green lacewings. Biweekly spraying of Garrett Juice is all that is usually needed long-term. Apply beneficial nematodes before bud break in the early spring.

TICKS

Ticks are difficult to control, but dusting with natural diatomaceous earth and using the flea program (see appendix) will control these pests. Bathing the pets regularly with herbal ingredients will help considerably.

WHITEFLIES

Whiteflies are very small and resemble little white moths. Whiteflies are extremely hard to control with chemicals and will suck the juices from several kinds of plants. They will attack vegetables and ornamental plants outdoors and indoors. Seaweed and garlic/pepper tea spray have been my most effective controls for infestations. However, beneficial insect populations will prevent the pest. Whiteflies have many natural enemies. Spray Garrett Juice plus orange oil.

ORGANIC PEST REMEDIES

APHIDS

Controls	Application
Water blast	Use hose nozzle or a strong thumb.
Garlic/pepper tea	Spray as needed.
Beneficial insects	Release ladybugs, braconid wasps, and green lacewings until a balanced population of bugs exists.

ANTS (Fire Ants, Carpenter Ants, and Pharoah Ants [Sugar])

Controls	Application
Garden-Ville Soil Conditioner	Mix of sugar and boric acid (for indoor use only).
Boric acid and sugar	Use in bait stations (indoors only).
Garrett Juice	Add 2 oz. of orange oil or d-limonene per gal. of water.
Tansy	Sprinkle bits of tansy leaf in problem area.
Baking soda	Dust indoors to control sugar ants.

BAGWORMS, CATERPILLARS, CORN BORERS, CABBAGEWORMS, ARMYWORMS

Controls	Application
Bt (*Bacillus thuringiensis*)	Spray with 1 tsp. soap per gal. at dusk.
Beneficial insects	Encourage and protect native wasps. Release green lacewings and trichogramma wasps.

Organic Pest Remedies (continued)

BEETLES (Elm leaf beetle, Flea beetle, and Borer beetle)

Controls	Application
Garden-VilleSoil conditioner	Make sure beetle in question is harmful—many are beneficial. Encourage biodiversity of insects, birds, plants, and small animals.
Neem	Use all per label instructions.
Citrus products	Use all per label instructions.

BORERS,TREE

Controls	Application
Wire	Run stiff wire into borer holes.
Nematodes	Put into holes full strength and moisten. Also treat the root zone per label directions.
Tree Trunk Goop	Apply to tree trunks as necessary.

CASEBEARERS

Controls	Application
Trichogramma wasp	Release eggs at least every 2 weeks starting with leaf emergence, usually mid-March.

CRICKETS, CHIGGERS, CHINCH BUGS

Controls	Application
Natural diatomaceous earth	Dust infested area @ 1 cup/1,000 sq. ft.
Garrett Juice plus orange oil	Add 2 oz. of orange oil concentrate per gal. of spray.
Nosema locustae (crickets - outside)	Broadcast on infested area.
Dusting sulfur (outside use)	Dust on legs to prevent chigger bites.

COLORADO POTATO BUG

Controls	Application
Bt 'San Diego'	Spray late in the day per label instructions.
Garlic/pepper tea and natural diatomaceous earth	Spray liquid mix as needed.

CUTWORMS

Controls	Application
Natural diatomaceous earth	Pour a ring of material around each plant.
Bone meal	Pour a ring of material around each plant.
Bt (*Bacillus thuringiensis*)	Apply per label at dusk. Add 1 tsp. liquid soap per gal.
Collars	Wrap aluminum foil around veggie stem.
Beneficial nematodes	Apply to the soil prior to planting.

Organic Pest Remedies (continued)

ELM LEAF BEETLE

Controls	Application
Horticulture oil	Spray per label for severe problems.
Garlic/pepper tea	¼ cup concentrate per gallon.
Bt (*Bacillus thuringiensis*)	Spray per label at dusk.
Garrett Juice plus orange oil	Add 2 oz. of orange oil concentrate per gal. of spray.

FLIES

Controls	Application
Garlic tea	Spray infested area.
Yellow sticky traps	Hang in infested area.
Tansy	Grind the herb and apply as a dry powder.
Natural diatomaceous earth	Add to livestock and pet food.
Fly parasites	Release as needed.

FLEA BEETLES

Controls	Application
Garrett Juice plus orange oil	Spray as needed. Add 2 oz. orange oil per gal.
Garlic tea/natural diatomaceous earth	Spray at first sign of problem.

FLEAS

Controls	Application
Garrett Juice plus orange oil	Spray as needed. Add 2 oz. of orange oil per gal. of water.
Citrus or d-limonene products	Follow label instructions.
Natural diatomaceous earth	Dust infested areas.
Garrett Juice	Add 2 oz. of orange oil or d-limonene per gal. of water.
Bathing	Bathe pets regularly in mild soapy water. Herbal shampoos are best.
Beneficial nematodes	Apply to soil per label directions. Critical step.

FUNGUS GNATS

Controls	Application
Baking soda spray	Spray lightly on soil.
Neem products	Apply per label instructions.
Water schedule	Allow soil to dry out between waterings.
Citrus oil spray	Spray the adults for a contact kill.

GRASSHOPPERS

Controls	Application
Nosema locustae products	Broadcast per label instructions when grasshoppers are young.
Hot pepper spray	Blast them as needed. Add garlic and citrus oil for more power.
Kaoline clay	Mix and spray with water and 1 tsp./gal. liquid soap.
Biodiversity	Plant heavily and use many species.
Birds	Feed, water, and attract as many as possible.

GRUBWORMS

Controls	Application
Beneficial nematodes	Release per label instructions.
All products that stimulate soil biology	Compost, organic fertilizers, microbial stimulators.
Sugar or dry molasses	Broadcast @ 5–10 lbs./1,000 sq.ft.

LACEBUGS

Controls	Application
Garlic/pepper tea	Spray liquid mix as needed.
Garrett Juice plus garlic tea	Add citrus oil for more power.
Horticultural oil/seaweed	Per label instructions.
Beneficial insects	Release praying mantises and ladybugs as necessary.

LEAFHOPPERS

Controls	Application
Garlic/pepper tea plus natural diatomaceous earth	Add the DE at 1 cup per gallon of spray.
Garrett Juice plus garlic tea	Add citrus oil for additional power.
Praying mantises	Release as necessary.

LEAFMINERS

Controls	Application
Neem	Spray per label instructions.
Don't worry about 'em	Minor damage only, usually no need to treat.
Spray Garrett Juice plus garlic tea	Omit the garlic once the infestation is reduced.

LOOPERS

Controls	Application
Bt (*Bacillus thuringiensis*)	Apply per label instructions at dusk.
Beneficial insects	Release regularly until healthy, native populations exist. Trichogramma wasps are the most effective.

MEALYBUGS

Controls	Application
Horticulture oil	Apply per label instructions. Add 1 tablespoon molasses per gallon of spray.
Mealybug predators	Release as needed
Lizards	Protect native ones and introduce new ones.

MITES

Controls	Application
Garrett Juice plus garlic	Spray as needed. Seaweed spray alone will also work.

MOSQUITOES

Controls	Application
Bti (*Bacillus thuringiensis* 'Israelensis')	Put briquettes or granules in standing water.
Encourage frogs, birds, bats	Eliminate standing, stagnant water.
Instant coffee	Sprinkle crystals in standing water.
Garlic oil	Apply top standing water.
Gambusia and goldfish	Small fish that love the taste of mosquitoe larvae.
Garlic/pepper tea	Spray for adult mosquitoes.
Citronella products	Spray as needed and use candles.
Cedar flakes	Broadcast on the surface of the soil.

MOTHS

Controls	Application
Bt (*Bacillus thuringiensis*)	Spray per label instructions at dusk. Add 1 tbs. molasses per gallon.
Beneficial insects	Release ladybugs and green lacewings every two weeks until natural control exists.

NEMATODES

Controls	Application
Organic matter	Stimulate soil biology with compost, organic fertilizers, and microbe stimulators.
Molasses	Apply dry material at 5–10 lbs./1,000 sq. ft.
Citrus	Apply orange and grapefruit pulp to soil prior to planting.

Organic Pest Remedies (continued)

PECAN CASE BEARER

Controls	Application
Trichogramma wasps	Release every 2 weeks during the spring. Start in mid-March at leaf emergence.
Green lacewings	Release as foliage starts to grow.
Bt (*Bacillus thuringiensis*)	Spray in early May. Add 1 ounce molasses per gallon of spray.

PILL BUGS (Sow Bugs)

Controls	Application
Beer traps	Plastic jar or dish sunk into ground.
Brewer's yeast and water traps	1 tbs. of yeast per gallon of water.
Bone meal or colloidal phosphate	Pour a ring around each plant.
Diatomaceous earth or wood ashes	Pour a ring around each plant.
Cedar flakes, hot pepper, natural DE	Dust around infested plants.

PLUM CURCULIO

Controls	Application
Garrett Juice plus garlic tea	Spray at pink bud, again after flowers have fallen.
Garlic/pepper tea	Spray during petal fall.
Mulch the tree's root system	Compost, shredded tree trimmings or alfalfa hay.
Tree Trunk Goop	Apply to tree trunks on injured limbs as needed.
* See appendix	

ROACHES

Controls	Application
Natural diatomaceous earth	Dust infested area lightly.
Boric acid	Dust infested areas lightly (indoors only).
Boric balls	Boric acid, flour, and sugar. Add water and roll into balls. Use indoors only.
Sugar and baking-soda detergent traps	1–2 tablespoons per bait station. See appendix.
Eliminate food sources	Remove food and water sources daily.
Citrus products	Spray as needed.

SCALE

Controls	Application
Dormant oil	Spray per label instructions in winter.
Horticultural oil	Spray per label instructions.
Beneficial insects	Release ladybugs and praying mantises.

Organic Pest Remedies (continued)

SQUASH BUGS

Controls	Application
Garden-Ville Soil Amendment	Spray per label on serious infestations.
Hand removal	Destroy copper colored eggs from the back side of leaves.
Bee balm (lemon balm)	Interplant with veggies.
All-purpose flour	Dust as needed.
Beneficial nematodes	Treat soil per label directions.

SQUASH VINE BORER

Controls	Application
Bt (*Bacillus thuringiensis*)	Spray very young plants and inject product into stem with syringe.
Beneficial insects	Release trichogramma wasps and green lacewings.
Beneficial nematodes	Treat soil per label instructions.

STINK BUGS

Controls	Application
Garrett Juice plus garlic tea	Spray per label instructions as needed.
Garlic/pepper tea/diatomaceous earth	Add DE to mix at 1 cup per gallon of water.

SLUGS, SNAILS

Controls	Application
Beer or brewer's yeast traps	Plastic jar or dish sunk into ground.
Garlic/pepper tea and natural diatomaceous earth	Spray as needed.
Natural diatomaceous earth	Dust infested area.
Bone meal or colloidal phosphate	Dust infested area or put ring around individual plants.
Encourage turtles	The real life kind.
Cedar flakes, natural DE, and hot pepper	Dust around plants as necessary.

SPIDERS

Controls	Application
Physically remove	No need to control spiders except black widow and brown recluse. The others are beneficial.
Citrus products	Spray orange oil or d-limonene products per label directions.

SOW BUGS (Pill bugs)-See Pill bugs

SPIDER MITES

Controls	Application
Beneficial insects	Release green lacewings and predatory mites.
Liquid seaweed	2 tbs./gal. Add citrus oil for extra effect.
Garlic/pepper tea	Spray every 3 days for 9 days.
Horticultural oil	Per label instructions. Last resort only.
Garrett Juice plus garlic tea	Spray as needed.

TERMITES

Controls	Application
Sand barrier	16-grit (00 sand blasting) sand placed around piers and grade beam or under the slab.
Boric acid	Follow label instructions for indoor use.
Beneficial nematodes	Apply to soil as preventative.
Citrus products	Spray on active infestations.

TICKS

Controls	Application
Natural diatomaceous earth	2 tbs./gal. Spray or dust infected area.
Garlic/pepper tea	Spray infected area.
Citrus products	Spray infected area as needed.
Beneficial nematodes	Apply to soil per label directions.

THRIPS

Controls	Application
Beneficial insects	Release green lacewings as needed.
Garlic/pepper tea	Spray every 2 weeks or as needed.
Garrett Juice plus garlic tea	Spray as needed.
Beneficial nematodes	Apply to soil before spring buds form.

TOBACCO HORN WORM

Controls	Application
Bt (*Bacillus thuringiensis*)	Spray per label instructions at dusk.
Beneficial insects	Release trichogramma and braconid wasps every 2 weeks.
Hand removal	There are usually only a few.

TOMATO PIN WORM

Controls	Application
Garlic/pepper tea	Spray every 2 weeks.
Garrett Juice plus garlic	Spray as needed.

TREEHOPPERS

Controls	Application
Garrett Juice plus garlic tea	Spray as needed.
Garlic/pepper tea	Spray every 2 weeks or as needed.

Organic Pest Remedies (continued)

WASPS

Controls	Application
Water blast (Protect if possible)	Nests can be moved to new location and nailed in place after spraying wasps with water. Do not attempt if allergic to wasps.
Citrus products	Spray to repel, not to kill.
Citronella products	Use per labe directions

WHITEFLIES

Controls	Application
Yellow sticky traps	Hang in infested area.
Beneficial insects	Release until natural populations exist.
Garden-Ville Fire Ant Control	Spray per label directions.
Garret Joice plus garlic tea	Spray as needed.

WEBWORMS

Controls	Application
Bt (*Bacillus thuringiensis*)	Spray with 1 oz. of milasses per gal. at dusk.
Wasps	Introduce and protect trichogramma wasps and natives.
Garden-Ville Fire Ant Control	Spray as needed.

DISEASES

ORGANIC DISEASE CONTROL

Disease control in an organic program is an interesting situation. Increased resistance to most diseases results as a nice side benefit from the use of organic products.

All organic products help control disease to some degree. When soil is healthy, there is a never-ending microscopic war being waged between the good and bad microorganisms, and the good guys usually win. Disease problems are simply situations where the microorganisms have gotten out of balance.

Drainage is a key ingredient for the prevention of diseases. Beds or tree pits that hold water and don't drain properly are the ideal breeding place for many disease organisms.

As with insects, spraying for diseases is only treating symptoms, not the major problems; plus, the toxic sprays kill more beneficials than the targeted pests. The primary cause of problems is usually related to the soil and the root system. Therefore it is critical to improve drainage, increase air circulation, add organic material, and stimulate and protect the living organisms in the soil.

ANTHRACNOSE: A serious fungal problem in sycamore trees, beans, and ornamentals where the foliage turns a tan color overnight. Control is difficult other than by avoiding susceptible plants. Bordeaux, baking soda, or potassium bicarbonate sprayed as leaves emerge in the spring will sometimes help. Best cure is soil improvement. Treat the soil with horticultural cornmeal and the overall Sick Tree Treatment.

BACTERIAL BLIGHT: A bacterial disease that causes dark-green water spots that turn brown and may die, leaving a hole in the leaves of tomatoes, plums, and several ornamental plants. Control includes healthy soil, baking-soda spray, garlic tea, and Consan 20 mix.

BLACK SPOT: Common name of fungal leaf spot. Black spot attacks the foliage of plants such as roses. There is usually a yellow halo around the dark spot. Entire leaves then turn yellow and ultimately die. Best controls include selection of resistant plants and Garrett Juice plus garlic tea and skim milk. Apply cornmeal to the soil.

BROWN PATCH: Cool-weather, fungal disease of St. Augustine. Brown leaves pull loose easily from the runners. Small spots in lawn grow into large circles that look bad and weaken the turf but rarely kill the grass. Soil health, drainage, and low nitrogen input are the best preventatives. Treat diseased turf with horticultural cornmeal at 10–20 lbs./1,000 sq. ft. Spray Garrett Juice plus potassium bicarbonate.

CANKER: A stress-related disease of trees and shrubs that causes decay of the bark and wood. Healthy soil and plants with strong immune systems are the solutions.

COTTON ROOT ROT: A fungal disease common in alkaline soils that attacks poorly adapted plants. The best preventative is healthy soil with a balance of nutrients and soil biology. Solutions include adding sulfur and sometimes sodium to the soil. Treat the soil with horticultural cornmeal at 10–20 lbs./1,000 sq. ft.

DAMPING OFF: A fungal disease of emerging seedlings where tiny plants fall over as if severed at the ground line. Avoid by using living (not sterilized) potting soil and by placing colloidal phosphate on the surface of planting media. Treat the soil with horticultural cornmeal.

ENTOMOSPORIUM: A fungal leaf spot disease of photinia, Indian hawthorne, and other plants that can be controlled by improving soil conditions and avoiding susceptible plants. This problem's real cause is a weak root system. Treat the plants with the Sick Tree Treatment in appendix.

FIREBLIGHT: Disease of plants in the rose family where twigs and limbs die back as though they've been burned. Leaves usually remain attached but often turn black or dark brown. Prune back into healthy tissue and disinfect pruning tools with 3 percent solution of hydrogen peroxide. Spray plants at first sign of disease with Garrett Juice plus garlic and potassium bicarbonate. Treat plants with the Sick Tree Treatment and cut back on the amount of nitrogen fertilizer.

GRAY LEAF SPOT: A disease of St. Augustine grass that forms gray vertical spots on the grass blades. A light baking-soda or potassium bicarbonate spray is the best curative. Prevent by improving soil health. Treat the soil with horticultural cornmeal at 10–20 lbs./1,000 sq. ft.

OAK WILT: A disease of the vascular system of oak trees which is transmitted through the air by insects and through the root system of neighboring trees by natural grafting. Biodiversity and soil health are the best deterrents. See the Sick Tree Treatment in the appendix. I do not recommend injecting toxic chemical fungicides into the tree. That only treats symptoms.

POWDERY MILDEW: White or gray, powdery, fungal growth on the leaf surface and flower buds of zinnias, crape myrtles, and many vegetables. Best control is Garrett Juice plus potassium bicarbonate. Treat the soil with horticultural cornmeal at 1–2 lbs./100 sq. ft.

SOOTY MOLD: Black fungal growth on the foliage of gardenias, crape myrtles, and other plants infested with aphids, scale, or whiteflies. It is caused by the honeydew (poop) of the insect pests. Best control is to release beneficial insects to control the pest bugs. Spray with Garrett Juice plus Neem or garlic tea.

ST. AUGUSTINE DECLINE: Virus in common St. Augustine grass that causes a yellow mottling. The grass slowly dies away. The answer is to replace turf with a healthier grass. The best St. Augustine at the moment is "Raleigh." Switching to the organic program will improve the long-term health of any grass.

ORGANIC DISEASE CONTROL

ANTHRACNOSE

Controls	Application
Potassium bicarbonate	Spray emerging foliage at 4 teaspoons per gal.
Better soil health	Use mulch, compost, rock powders, biostimulants.
Sick Tree Treatment	See appendix.

BACTERIAL BLIGHT

Controls	Application
Hydrogen peroxide	Spray as needed mixed with Garrett Juice.
Garlic/pepper tea	Spray as needed per label instructions.
Better soil health	Use mulch, compost, rock powders, and biostimulants.
Garrett Juice plus garlic tea	Spray as needed.

BLACK SPOT (Fungal leaf spot)

Control	Application
Potassium bicarbonate	Spray lightly as needed. Potassium bicarbonate is better.
Better soil health	Use mulch, compost, rock powders, biostimulants.
Garrett Juice plus garlic tea	Add skim milk for even more power.
Cornmeal	Apply to soil at 20 lbs./1,000 sq. ft.

BROWN PATCH

Controls	Application
Horticultural cornmeal	Apply at 10–20 lbs./1,000 sq. ft.
Better soil health	Mulch, compost, rock powders, biostimulants. Avoid wet soil and high-nitrogen fertilizers.
Garrett Juice plus potassium bicarbonate	Spray as needed.

CANKER

Controls	Application
Increase drainage	Change planting site, aerate soil mulch.
Delay pruning until bud swell	Never make flush cuts or use pruning paint.
Better soil health	Mulch, compost, rock powders, biostimulants. Use the Sick Tree Treatment.

FIREBLIGHT

Controls	Application
Garlic/pepper tea	Spray plants while in bloom.
Better soil health	Mulch, compost, rock powders, biostimulants.
Limit use of nitrogen	Cut off infected area.
Garrett Juice plus garlic	Add potassium bicarbonate for additional power.
Hydrogen peroxide	Can be added to any of the above mixes.

GRAY LEAF SPOT

Controls	Application
Potassium bicarbonate	Light foliage spray as needed.
Better soil health	Aerate and balance the soil nutrients.
Garrett Juice plus garlic tea	Spray as needed.
Cornmeal	Broadcast at 20 lbs./1,000 sq. ft.

OAK WILT

Controls	Application
Maintain soil and plant health	Fertilize with organic techniques, and water regularly.
Sick Tree Treatment	See appendix.

POWDER MILDEW

Controls	Application
Baking-soda spray	Light foliage spray as needed. Potassium bicarbonate is better.
Better soil health	Use mulch, compost, rock powders, biostimulants.
Garrett Juice plus garlic	Spray as needed.
Horticultural cornmeal	Broadcast at 20 lbs./1,000 sq. ft.

PEACH TREE CURL

Controls	Application
Baking-soda spray	Spray in fall. Potassium bicarbonate is better.
Garrett Juice plus garlic tea	Spray in fall.
Better soil health	Use mulch, compost, rock powders, and biostimulants.
Sick Tree Treatment	See appendix.

SOOTY MOLD

Controls	Application
Baking-soda spray	Light spray as needed. Potassium bicarbonate is better.
Beneficial insects	Ladybugs and green lacewings will control aphids whose honeydew causes the sooty mold.
Garrett Juice plus garlic tea	Spray as needed.

TAKE-ALL-PATCH

Controls	Application
Horticultural cornmeal	Apply at 20 lbs./1,000 sq. ft.
Apple cider vinegar	Spray at 2 oz./gal.

Note:

Since the last edition, I have gotten smart enough to stop recommending all copper based products. Copper is a heavy metal that is needed in very small amounts in the soil, but can very easily accumulate to toxic levels.

WEEDS

Have you ever read anything good about the weeds? Unless you've read Malcolm Beck's *Lessons in Nature* or Charles Walters' *Weeds*, probably not!

Weeds are Nature's greatest and most diverse group of plants. Even though many members of the weed fraternity are beautiful, man has been convinced by the chemical poison fraternity to condemn the weeds and consider them his enemy. Mention weeds and most people think in terms of control through spraying toxic pesticides. They rarely think of why the weeds grow or of their value.

Weeds are here on earth for very specific purposes. Different weeds have different jobs to do. Some are here to ensure that the soil always has the protection of a green blanket to shade and cool the ground. Others are here to prevent the erosion of bare soil. Others are here to help balance the minerals in the soil. Many weeds provide all these important functions.

Weeds take no chances. They germinate and spread to protect any soil left bare by man's mismanagement of the land. In every cubic foot of soil lie millions of weed seeds waiting to germinate when needed. When man strips the green growth off the land, weeds are needed. When hard winters freeze the ornamental lawn grasses, weeds are needed. When we mow too low and apply harsh chemicals to the soil, weeds are needed.

If it weren't for weeds, the topsoil of the earth would have eroded away years ago. Much of the topsoil has already gone from our farms forever to muddy our rivers and fill our lakes and eventually end up in our oceans.

It's a common misunderstanding that weeds rob our crops of moisture, sunlight, and nutrients. Weeds only borrow water and nutrients and eventually return it all to the soil for future crop use.

Weeds are tough. Rarely do you find weeds destroyed by insects or disease. Some weeds are pioneer plants, as they are able to grow in soil unsuited for edible or domesticated plants. Weeds are able to build the soil with their strong and powerful roots that go deep, penetrating and loosening hard-packed soil. The deep roots bring minerals, especially trace elements, from the subsoil to the topsoil.

Weeds are indicators of certain soil deficiencies and actually collect or manufacture certain mineral elements that are lacking in the soil. This is Nature's wonderful way of buffering and balancing the chemistry of soil.

Some weeds are good companion plants. Some have insect-repelling abilities, while others with deep roots help surface-feeding plants obtain moisture during dry spells. Weeds act as straws to bring water up from the deep, moist soil so that shallow-rooted plants can get some of the moisture.

Control becomes necessary when the vigorous weeds become too numerous in the fields and gardens. However, not understanding the dangers of spraying chemicals into the environment, farmers, gardeners, and landscape people have primarily used powerful toxic herbicides. Most herbicides upset or unbalance the harmony of the soil organisms, and some herbicides can persist in the soil for months or longer. Even though microbes can repopulate after chemical treatment damage, they are slow to reestablish the complicated, natural balance.

There are safe and nonpolluting weed control methods such as mechanically aerating, mulching with organic materials, and using organic fertilizers to stimulate the growth of more desirable plants. The old, reliable methods of hand weeding, hoeing, and timely cultivating are not yet against the law and are good exercise.

The best weed control in turf is the following: Water deeply but infrequently, fertilize with natural organic fertilizers, mow at a higher setting, and leave the clippings on the ground. Easy and effective weed control in the ornamental and vegetable beds is done by keeping a thick blanket of mulch on the bare soil at all times. Clover, wild violets, and other herbs and wildflowers should sometimes be encouraged. Many plants that start out looking like noxious weeds end up presenting beautiful flower displays and wonderful fragrances. They're called wildflowers.

Weed control starts with a new attitude about weeds. A few are acceptable, even beneficial.

ORGANIC HERBICIDE: Full strength vinegar (10 percent acidity or greater) with 2 ounces of orange oil or d-limonene and 1 tablespoon of liquid soap per gallon. Do not dilute.

ORGANIC WEED CONTROL

WEEDS (general)

Controls	Application
Vinegar/citrus products	Spray as needed.
Chop with a hoe or hand remove	This is still legal.
Accept a few	Many "weeds" are herbs, wildflowers, and beneficial
Burn Out	Spray as needed.
Garden-Ville Weed control	Spray as needed.

BERMUDAGRASS, ST. AUGUSTINE

Controls	Application
Vinegar/citrus products	Spray as needed.
Dig out	Use a sod cutter or hoe to remove rhizomes and stolons.
Burn Out	Spray as needed.
Garden-Ville Weed control	Spray as needed.

Pest Control

Organic Weed Control (continued)

NUTGRASS

Controls	Application
Ryegrass	Overseed turf areas.
Mulch	Cover weeds in beds with a thick blanket of mulch.
Hand remove	Dig out infested area and sift through wire mesh to catch the nutlets and roots.
Chemical products	Avoid like the plague. They injure and kill trees.

JOHNSONGRASS

Controls	Application
Physically remove	Can't stand to be mowed or regularly cut down.

CRABGRASS

Controls	Application
Fertilizer	Crabgrass can't stand fertility.
Mowing height	Mow at a height of 3" or more.
Citrus-vinegar products	Spray as needed.

DALLISGRASS

Controls	Application
Cornmeal	Apply ¼" over the entire weed and water. Molasses also works to rot the crown. Dig out later.
Physical removal	Dig out with mechanical tools.
Vinegar/citrus products	Spray prior to physical removal.
MSMA	This toxic product recommended by organiphobes is far too toxic. The "A" stands for arsenic.

POISON IVY

Controls	Application
Physically remove plants	Do not attempt if you are highly allergic. Protect skin.
Vinegar/citrus products	Spray young growth as it emerges.
Comfrey juice.	Apply to skin to prevent or to relieve rash pain.

POND ALGAE

Controls	Application
Tilapia fish*	Release in spring after water temperature is above 60°.
Water circulation	Circulating water with pump or fountain.
Cornmeal	Broadcast across water surface at 5 lbs./1,000 sq. ft. 150 lbs. per surface acre.

POND WEEDS

Organic Solution	Application
White Amur fish*	Release in spring after water temperature is above 60°.

*License for both these fish available through fish and wildlife departments.

MISCELLANEOUS ORGANIC CONTROL

STUPID NEIGHBORS

Control	Application
Try to help them or move	Give them the names of organic books to read; ask them to tune in to *The Natural Way* on WBAP, 820 AM, from 8–12 on Sunday mornings and read "The Natural Way" in The *Dallas Morning News* on Friday.

ALLERGIES

Control	Application
Mint and honey tea	10 cups of water, 5 sprigs spearmint, 2 applemint, 2 bee balm, 1 peppermint, 1 tablespoon honey, and a slice of lemon. Steep—don't boil, drink, and enjoy.
Aloe vera	Aloe Vera (Manapol) tablets from Carrington Labs.

ORGANIC ANIMAL CONTROL

ARMADILLOS

Control	Application
Live traps	Piper™ or Havahart™. Need to use batter boards to form a "V" to guide them into the trap.

BIRDS

Control	Application
Cats	I'd rather have the birds.
Soapy water	Last resort: spray roosting birds with mild liquid soap solution. Do in warm weather only.
Garlic/pepper spray	Most birds are beneficial and a natural mix of life in the garden will usually control populations.

CATS

Control	Application
Dogs	Or keep the cats indoors.
Citrus extract or peelings	Apply to problem areas.
Live traps	Pied Piper™ or Havahart™.
Dry cayenne or other hot pepper	Spread around problem area.
Rose cuttings	Spread any thorny cuttings in beds.
Citronella	Spray as needed.

Pest Control

Organic Animal Control (continued)

DEER

Control	Application
Hinder™	Apply per label directions.
Soap bar	Hang in trees in problem areas.
Blood meal	Spread around problem areas.
Human hair	Put in porous bags.
Liquid Fence	Apply per label directions.

DOGS

Control	Application
Live traps	Pied Piper™ or Havahart™.
Dog runs	It is not cruel to house dogs in dog runs when not at home.
Dog-B-Gone	1 part cayenne pepper, 2 parts mustard powder, 2 parts flour, or use straight cayenne or other hot pepper.
Hot pepper	Dust as needed.

GOPHERS

Control	Application
Black Hole Gopher Trap™	Install in tunnel per instructions.
Gopher spurge	Plant gopher spurge (*Euphobia lathyrus*) around the perimeter of problem area.
Caster bean plants	Plant as a barrier to garden areas.
Garlic	Plant as a barrier to garden areas.
Other metal traps	Install in tunnels per instructions.
Hot pepper/castor oil	Inject in the problem areas and spray on surface.
Noisy devices	Install windmills or rattling devices.

MICE

Control	Application
Cats	Hope you aren't allergic.
Traps	Still looking for a better one.
Baits	Apply in bait stations.
Cats	The natural way.
Peppermint	Use ground-up pieces of mint or cardboard soaked in peppermint oil as repellent.
Fox urine	Apply per label directions.

MOLES

Control	Application
Same as for gophers	At least you have nice, sandy soil.

Organic Animal Control (continued)

RABBITS

Control	Application
Low and recessed fences	Electric fences are even better.
Cayenne or other pepper	Dust onto problem area.
Blood meal	Spread around problem area.
Fox urine	Apply per label directions.
Liquid Fence™	Apply per label directions.

RACCOONS

Control	Application
Live traps	Pied Piper™ or Havahart™.
Garlic/pepper tea	Spray as needed.

RATS

Control	Application
Death traps	Still looking for a better one.
Live traps	Pied Piper™ or Havahart™.
Bait stations	Rampage or Quintox per label directions.
Fox urine	Apply as needed.

SKUNKS

Control	Application
Live traps	Pied Piper™ or Havahart™.
	Be careful of the spray and bites. Many skunks are rabid.
Fox urine	Apply as needed.

SNAKES

Control	Application
Introduce bull and king snakes	These guys look fierce but are great friends.
Roadrunners, guineas, and other snake-eating birds	They control the dangerous snakes like rattlers, copperheads, coral, and water moccasins.
Most garden snakes are beneficial	Protect Nature's biodiversity.
Citronella	Spray as needed.

SQUIRRELS

Control	Application
Live traps	Pied Piper™ or Havahart™.
Fox urine	Apply to problem areas. Works as a repellent.
Blood meal and/or cayenne or other hot pepper	Spread around problem area.

TURTLES

Control	Application
Underwater traps for aquatic turtles	Pied Piper™.
Land turtles are mostly beneficial	Fence off vegetable garden.

PRODUCTS

ORGANIC FERTILIZERS

One of the biggest problems with synthetic fertilizers is that they contain no organic matter and therefore there is no carbon. Soil microorganisms must have this carbon energy source and if it is not provided, the microbes will take it from the soil. That causes soil health reduction with every fertilizer application.

Organic fertilizers nourish and improve the soil. As opposed to synthetic fertilizers, they help the soil because they do not create high levels of salts and nitrates in the soil, which kill or repel beneficial soil organisms. Organic fertilizers release nutrients slowly and naturally. All components in an organic fertilizer are usable by the plants, since there are no useless fillers as in synthetic fertilizers.

The nitrogen-phosphorus-potassium analysis (N-P-K) printed on bags of fertilizer by law is basically irrelevant in an organic program. Feeding the soil and plants with nothing but nitrogen, phosphorus, and potassium is like feeding your kids nothing but cheese. Soil and people need a balance of nutrients. For some unknown reason, fertilizer recommendations continue to emphasize these three nutrients with special emphasis on high levels of nitrogen. A standard obsolete recommendation is a ratio of 3–1–2 or 4–1–2, such as 15–5–10 or 16–4–8.

Studies have shown that as much as 50 percent of all synthetic nitrogen applied to the soil will be leached out, and the half that does reach the

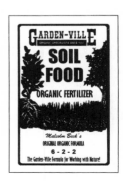

plant may be harmful. Other studies show that an excess of chemical fertilizer slows or even stops the activity of micro flora and micro fauna such as beneficial bacteria, algae, fungi, and other microorganisms. Harsh fertilizers also cause damage to macro organisms, such as earthworms, millipedes, centipedes, etc., which are extremely important to the natural processes in the soil.

High-nitrogen fertilizers also can cause severe thatch buildup in lawns by forcing unnatural flushes of green growth. That's why mechanical thatch removal programs are often recommended for chemically maintained lawns. Organic lawn care programs take care of thatch problems naturally as the living microorganisms feed on the grass clippings and other dead organic matter.

High-nitrogen fertilizers such as 15–5–10 (or even higher) are still being recommended by many in the farming, ranching, and landscaping business. I've made the same recommendations myself in the past, but those amounts of nitrogen, phosphorus, and potassium are unnecessary and even damaging to soil health.

When healthy, the soil will produce and release nutrients during the decomposition process. The microbiotic activity releases tied up trace elements such as iron, zinc, boron, chlorine, copper, magnesium, molybdenum, and others, which are all important to a well-balanced soil.

The most important material in an organic program is organic matter, which becomes humus during the decomposition process. Humus becomes humic acid, other beneficial acids, and mineral nutrients.

Organic fertilizers are better than artificial products because they are the derivatives of plants and therefore contain most or all the trace elements that exist in growing plants, probably all 92 basic elements. Synthetic fertilizers do not have this rounded balance of mineral nutrients.

In addition, organic fertilizers are naturally slow release and provide nutrients to plants when they need the nutrients. Synthetic fertilizers glut the plants with nutrients immediately after application, which is usually at the wrong time.

ORGANIC FERTILIZERS AND SOIL AMENDMENTS

ALFALFA MEAL: Alfalfa provides many nutritional benefits not only for plant use, but for soil organisms as well. One very important ingredient is triacontanol, a powerful plant growth regulator. Orchid and rose growers make alfalfa tea and spray it directly on as a foliar fertilizer. Alfalfa is very high in vitamins, plus N-P-K, calcium, magnesium, and other valuable minerals. It also includes sugars, starches, proteins, fiber, and 16 amino acids. Use at 10–20 lbs./1,000 sq. ft.

ALFALFA TEA: In a 5-gallon bucket, put 1 cup alfalfa meal. Fill bucket with water and let it sit overnight. The result will be a thick tea. Apply generously to the root area of shrubs and flowers or use as a foliar spray after straining.

BAT GUANO: A natural, all-purpose fertilizer containing nitrogen and lots of trace elements. The analysis will vary with the age of the guano. It has natural fungicidal qualities and has almost no chance of being contaminated with pesticides or chemicals. It is an excellent supplemental fertilizer for flowers. Best to apply once or twice during the growing season. It looks mild but has as much as 10 percent nitrogen, so be careful not to overuse.

BIOFORM: Excellent liquid fertilizer made from fish emulsion, seaweed, and molasses. The analysis is 4–2–4–3S. The sulfur in the molasses has greatly reduced the fish smell. The product contains a biostimulant/ soil penetrant.

Liquid products that contain fish, seaweed, molasses and dry products that contain poultry manure and other natural ingredients, such as Bioform 4–2–4 with 3 percent sulfur for lawns: 2 to 4 quarts per acre, diluted in 20 gallons water (water well). For all other: 4 tablespoons per gallon of water (mist). Bioform Dry 5–3–4 with 1 percent sulfur. 40 pound bag covers approximately 2,000 square feet (water well).

BLOOD MEAL: Organic source of nitrogen and phosphorus. Good to use as a mix with cottonseed meal. Expensive but good to use occasionally. Analysis can range from 12–2 to 11–0–0. Does have a strong odor.

BONE MEAL: Source of calcium and phosphorus recommended for bulbs, tomatoes, and other vegetables. Analysis will range from 2–12–0 to 4–12–0 with 2 percent to 5 percent calcium. Soft rock phosphate is better and cheaper.

BRADFIELD: Approximate analysis is 3–1–5. Bradfield's natural fertilizers are alfalfa-based fertilizers blended with animal protein, natural potassium sulfate potash, and molasses. They should be used at the rate of 20–30 pounds per 1,000 square feet. Most broadcast spreaders, set fully open, will dispense this fertilizer at approximately 10 pounds per 1,000 square feet per pass.

CATTLE MANURE: Manure is one of our greatest natural resources. It has to be handled properly and not overused in any one area. Using too much of anything can cause problems. Manure can be properly used in several ways. Cow manure is a good ingredient for the manufacture of compost or for use directly on agricultural fields. Dairy cow manure is best because it has the least chance of chemical contamination. It should be composted prior to using in the home vegetable garden.

CEDAR FLAKES: Good for chiggers, fleas, and lowering the pH of the soil. An excellent material to use on the floor of greenhouses. Cedar flakes are an excellent control for harmful nematodes. Would be a staple organic product today if A&M hadn't sabotaged it.

CHELATORS: Chelated iron and other chelated nutrients are used when a direct dose of a particular nutrient is needed to quickly solve a deficiency. Chelated products are organic compounds with attached inorganic metal molecules, which are more available for plant use. Compost, humus, humic acid, and microorganisms have natural chelating properties.

CHICKEN LITTER: Chicken litter is a good natural fertilizer high in nitrogen. Pelletized forms are better because they are not as dusty. Approximate analysis is 6–4–2. Unfortunately, commercial chickens are still being fed lots of unnatural things including arsenic. Best to compost before using.

COMPOST: The best fertilizer and the key to any organic program. Nature's own product, high in nutrients, humus, humic acid, and microorganisms. Compost has magical healing and growing powers and can be used successfully on any and all plants. Analysis will vary due to ingredients. Compost can be made at home or purchased commercially. The best composts are those made from a variety of organic material such as hay, sawdust, paunch manure, leaves, twigs, bark, wood chips, dead plants, food scraps, pecan hulls, grass clippings, and animal manure. The best manure to use is whatever is locally available: chicken, turkey, cattle, horse, rabbit, etc.

COTTONSEED MEAL: A good natural fertilizer with an acid pH. Analysis will vary and ranges from 6–2–1 to 7–2–2 with trace elements. Does have odor, but is a good organic source of nitrogen. As of this printing there is no good source of organically grown cottonseed meal.

EARTHWORM CASTINGS: An effective organic fertilizer that is high in bacteria, calcium, iron, magnesium, and sulfur as well as N-P-K and has over 60 trace minerals. Earthworm castings make an excellent ingredient in potting soil, in flats when germinating seed, and to toss into each hole when planting vegetables, herbs, or small ornamentals. It is a gentle, sweet-smelling and clean organic fertilizer. Excellent for interior plants.

FISH EMULSION: A concentrated liquid fish fertilizer for use directly in the soil or as a foliar feed. The analysis will range from 4–1–1 to 5–2–2. It is reported to be an effective insecticide. Good all-purpose spray when mixed with liquid kelp. Has an odor for about 24 hours—a pretty strong one, in fact.

FISH MEAL: A natural fertilizer originally used in this country by Native Americans growing corn. They used whole fish. Has a high analysis of approximately 8–12–2, but is also stinky, so use with caution. Very good for flowering plants.

GARDEN-VILLE SOIL FOOD: Organic fertilizer made in San Antonio by compost maker Malcolm Beck. Approximate analysis is 6–2–2. This is an organic fertilizer for gardens and lawns containing bat guano, brewer's yeast, desert humate, Norwegian kelp, compost, fish meal, meat and bone meal, molasses and langbeinite, cottonseed meal, blood meal, and alfalfa meal. Use at 20–30 pounds per 1,000 square feet. 7-2-2 is an economical biosolids product.

GARRETT JUICE: Garrett Juice is a subtly powerful foliar feeding spray. It can be used as a liquid soil fertilizer as well. For foliar feeding, use it with water at 2–3 ounces per gallon and use on herbs, vegetables, groundcover, shrubs, vines, trees, turf grasses, and greenhouse plants. Garrett Juice is a blend of manure compost tea, seaweed, apple cider vinegar, and molasses. It can be used on any age plants, but it's always best to spray any liquid materials during the cooler parts of the day. For soil treatment, the application rate can be doubled. Garrett Juice provides major nutrients, trace minerals and other beneficial components. See appendix for recipe.

GLAUCONITE: See Texas Greensand

GRANITE SAND: Sand-like residue from the granite quarry or natural deposits. Excellent way to add minerals to planting beds. Much better than washed concrete sand. Contains 5 percent potash and many trace minerals. Also has paramagnetism.

GREENSENSE: Approximate analysis is 5–2–4. GreenSense Dairy, all-purpose lawn and garden fertilizer, is an odor-free fertilizer made from composted dairy manure, cottonseed meal, corn gluten meal, and more. A bag contains 40 pounds; apply 10–20 pounds per 1,000 square feet.

Another GreenSense product is a poultry lawn and garden fertilizer, which has an analysis of 6–2–4. It is granular fertilizer rich from composted poultry manure, blood meal, bone meal and more. Apply 10–20 pounds per 1,000 square feet 40 pounds per bag.

GYPSUM: This natural material is calcium sulfate and is an excellent source of calcium and sulfur. Gypsum also neutralizes plant toxins, removes sodium from the soil, and opens the soil structure to promote aeration and drainage. Gypsum is approximately 23 percent calcium and 17 percent sulfate. It is not needed in high calcium soils.

HORSE MANURE: Horse manure is higher in nitrogen than most other farm animal manures and is an excellent material to use for the manufacture of compost. Fresh manures should not be tilled directly into the soil unless they are applied a month before planting or composted first. Sheep manure has similar properties and uses.

HUMATES: Leonardite shale is basically low-grade lignite coal and is an excellent source of carbon, humic acid, and trace minerals. Percentage of humic acid, will vary. May be made into liquid form or used in the dry form.

HYDROGEN PEROXIDE: An oxidizing liquid for use on soil in diluted amounts. A dangerous product in concentrated forms.

KELP MEAL: A dry fertilizer made from seaweed. Approximate analysis is 1–0–8 with lots of trace minerals, and plant hormones which stimulate root growth and regulate plant growth. Seaweed also provides soil-conditioning substances, improves the soil crumb structure, or tilth, and helps stimulate microorganisms.

LAVA SAND: The sand-sized and smaller waste material left from lava gravel is an excellent, highly paramagnetic soil-amendment material. It can be used in potting soils and bed preparation for all landscaping and food crops. Finer textured material would be even better if it was easily available.

LEATHER TANKAGE: Leather tankage is a slaughter house by-product high in nitrogen. Several organic fertilizers are derived from leather tankage. Some tankage contains toxic chemicals used in the tanning process.

LIME: A major calcium fertilizer, dolomitic lime contains 30–35 percent magnesium. High-calcium lime is preferred because most low calcium soils have plenty of magnesium. High calcium lime is calcium carbonate.

MAESTRO-GRO: A high quality line of organic fertilizers that include a wide variety of ingredients such as bone meal, fish meal, feather meal, rock phosphates, kelp meal, greensand, molasses and microorganisms. Maestro-Gro liquids are also available for foliar feeding and pest control.

MEDINA: Approximate analysis is 6–12–6. Hasta Gro is a Medina product that combines organic materials such as seaweed with urea.

MILORGANITE: Sewer-sludge fertilizer from Milwaukee. Has been widely used on golf courses. Many cities now make a similar product. Hou-Actinite is a biosolid product made in Houston.

MOLASSES: Sweet syrup that is a carbohydrate used as a soil amendment to feed and stimulate microorganisms. Contains sulfur, potash, and many trace minerals. Liquid molasses is used in sprays and dry molasses is used as an ingredient in organic fertilizers.

RABBIT MANURE: The average analysis of rabbit manure is around 2.5–1.5–5. Mixed with leaves, sawdust, straw, grass, and other vegetative materials, it makes an excellent compost. Can be used directly as a fertilizer without fear of burning plants. Llama and Alpaca manures can also be used directly without composting first.

ROOT STIMULATORS: This is a generic term that refers to mild fertilizers or any material that stimulates microbial activity and root growth. Liquid seaweed, vinegar, molasses, and compost tea also function as root stimulators. Most commercial root stimulators are simply liquid synthetic fertilizers and shouldn't be used.

SEAWEED: Best used as a foliar spray. Excellent source of trace minerals. Should be used often. Contains hormones that stimulate root growth and branching. Many trace elements are found in seaweed in the proportions they are found in plants. Seaweed contains hormones and functions as a mild but effective insect control, especially for whiteflies and spider mites. It acts as a chelating agent, making other fertilizers and nutrients more available to the plants. Seaweed or kelp is available in liquid and in dry meals.

SEWER SLUDGE: Processed human waste. Most cities produce this product. It is an excellent lawn fertilizer and should be used more often.

SOFT ROCK PHOSPHATE: A mixture of fine particles of phosphate suspended in a clay base. Economic form of natural phosphorus and calcium. Unlike chemically made phosphates, soft rock phosphate is insoluble in water, will not leach away, and therefore is long-lasting. Has 18 percent phosphorus and 15 percent calcium as well as trace elements. Florida is the primary source.

SUL-PO-MAG: A naturally occurring mineral containing 22 percent sulfur, 22 percent potash, and 11.1 percent magnesium. An excellent product for the organic program.

SULFUR: A basic mineral often lacking in alkaline soils. Applying granulated sulfur at 5 lbs./1,000 sq. ft. twice annually can bring base saturation of calcium down and raise magnesium. Be careful not to breathe the dust, over-apply, or use when planting seed. It can act as a preemergent. Sulfur dust is also used as a pesticide in some situations.

SUPERTHRIVE: A liquid product made from vitamins and hormones. It is a good supplement for flowering plants. Use at 3 drops per gallon at each watering for best results. It can be mixed with other products.

SUSTANE: A manufactured fertilizer made from composted turkey manure and other natural materials. It is granulated and has some odor for 24–36 hours and has shown excellent soil improvement and reduction of diseases.

TEXAS GREENSAND: A material called glauconite, which is a naturally deposited undersea, iron-potassium silicate. It's an excellent source of iron and other trace minerals with a normal analysis of about 0–1–5. It's best used with other fertilizers and organic materials. Contains 19 to 20 percent iron. Jersey greensand or high calcium lime is a better choice for people with acid soils.

TURKEY MANURE: Turkey manure is a high-nitrogen product that is an excellent ingredient for compost making. It is too "hot" to use direct unless planting is delayed for several weeks.

ZEOLITE: Volcanic material that is used for bed preparation and soil detoxification. Zeolite especially likes to grab excess ammonia. That's how it works as an air purifier. It will also lock up certain heavy metals. It is a good ingredient for potting soil.

ZINC: A trace mineral that is an important fertilizer element for pecans and other crops. Will defoliate fruit trees if overused. It is not needed in acid soils or balanced soils. Spraying or soil applying raw zinc products regularly is not recommended. Zinc is a trace element found in most organic fertilizers.

> The definition of a good organic product is this: "Any material that when applied improves the balance and health of the soil."

FERTILIZER CHART (Generic Products)

Organic Fertilizers	N	P	K*	Comments
Alfalfa	3	1	2	Vitamin A, folic acid, trace minerals, and growth hormone "tricontanol."
Bat guano	10	3	1	High in nitrogen, phosphorus, and trace minerals.
Blood meal	12	1	1	Good nitrogen source but smelly.
Bone meal	2	12	0	Good calcium and phosphorus, calcium, and trace minerals.
Cow manure	2	1	1	Best all-around organic fertilizer.
Colloidal phosphate	0	18	0	Excellent organic source of phosphorus, calcium, and trace minerals.
Compost	1	1	1	Best all-around organic fertilizer.
Cottonseed meal	7	2	2	Acid pH, lots of trace minerals.
Earthworm castings	1	.1	.1	Beneficial bacteria, trace minerals, humus, earthworm eggs.
Fish emulsion	5	2	2	Foliar plant food, helps with insect control, stinks!
Fish meal	7	13	3	Nitrogen, phosphorus, and lots of vitamins and minerals but smelly.
Granite sand	0	0	5	Low cost source of minerals, especially potash.
Greensand	0	2	5	Natural source of phosphorus, and lots of vitamins and minerals but smelly.
Horse manure	4	1	1	More powerful than cow manure.
Molasses	1	0	5	Food for microorganisms and source of sulfur and potash.
Rabbit manure	3	2	1	Not used enough, excellent source of natural nutrition.
Pig manure	.5	.3	.5	Good source of humus and micro-organisms.
Poultry manure	5	3	2	High-nitrogen organic fertilizer, best to compost first.
Sheep manure	.5	.3	5	Good natural fertilizer.
Seaweed (dry)	1	0	1	Trace minerals and hormones that stimulate root growth and branching.
Seaweed (liquid)	1	0	1	Trace minerals and hormones that stimulate root growth and branching.
Sludge compost	5	3	0	Same as dry but can be used as a foliar spray.
Sul-Po-Mag	0	0	22	Mined source of sulfur, potassium, and magnesium.
Tankage	6	8	0	Slaughter house by-product.

*The analysis of organic fertilizers will vary depending on the raw ingredients and the processing.

MANUFACTURED FERTILIZERS

Organic Fertilizers	N	P	K	Comments
Bioform	4	2	4	Fish emulsion, seaweed, and molasses.
GreenSense	3	1	2	Composted manure, activated carbon, alfalfa, molasses, ferrous sulfate.
Garden-Ville Soil Food	6	2	2	Compost, humate, bat guano, cottonseed meal.
Maestro-Gro	6	2	4	Fish meal, bone meal, and other natural ingredients.
Sustane	5	2	4	Composted turkey manure.
Hou-Actinite	6	3	0	Sludge product from Houston.
Bradfield	3	1	5	Alfalfa meal, molasses, potassium sulfate and poultry meal.

FOLIAR FEEDING

Feeding the soil is the basis of organics. However, there are ways of stimulating the natural processes in the soil and in the plants without putting the material into the soil. Spraying the foliage of plants can provide some significant horticultural advantages.

Some foliar sprays such as fish emulsion, compost tea, humate, and seaweed are fertilizers. When fertilizer nutrients are sprayed directly on the foliage, immediate results can often be seen because the micronutrients, when taken in through the foliage, are immediately available to the plant.

When food crops or ornamentals have a chlorotic symptom (yellow leaves with green veins) resulting from lack of iron, magnesium, or other soil elements, spraying the foliage with a chelated product can create a greening improvement within a few days. Organic products have natural chelating abilities. Plants need green foliage to be able to produce food through the process of photosynthesis where sunlight, water, and carbon dioxide combine in the leaves to produce sugars and carbohydrates to feed the plant.

Some spray products are stimulators rather than feeders. They work by stimulating plant growth and flower/fruit production by increasing photosynthesis in the foliage, increasing the movement of fluids and energy within the plant, increasing root exudates and microbiotic activity in the soil at the root zone, and increasing the uptake of nutrients from the soil through the root hairs. In other words, foliar feeding can provide missing or "locked up" elements as well as stimulate all of the natural systems in the plant and in the soil. The end result is bigger, stronger, healthier plants with increased drought, insect, and disease resistance.

Here are some points to remember when using foliar sprays:

1 Less is usually better in foliar sprays. Light, regularly applied sprays are better than heavy, infrequent blasts. Mists of liquids are better than big drops, unless you are also trying to control pests.

2 High humidity increases a leaf's ability to absorb sprays. Spraying on damp mornings or evenings will increase the effectiveness of the spray. The small openings (stomata) on the leaves close up during the heat of the day so that moisture within the plant is preserved. The best time of day to spray is late afternoon for pest control. Daybreak is best for foliar feeding.

3 Young foliage seems to absorb nutrients better than old, hard foliage. Therefore, foliar feeding is most effective during the periods of new growth on plants.

4 Adding sugar or molasses in small amounts to your spray solutions can stimulate the growth of beneficial microorganisms on the leaf surfaces. The stimulation of friendly microbes helps to fight off the harmful pathogens.

5 Foliar feeding will increase the storage life of food crops. It will also increase cold and heat tolerance.

Organic foliar feedings can help control insects and disease as well as fertilize and stimulate plants. The best foliar feeding spray is Garrett Juice, a mix of compost tea, natural apple cider vinegar, liquid seaweed, and blackstrap molasses. See the appendix for the exact recipe.

Foliar feeding has been used since 1844 when it was discovered that plant nutrients could be leached from leaves by rain. Experiments soon proved that nutrients could also enter the plant through the foliage. It's still somewhat of a mystery as to just exactly how the nutrients enter the plant through the foliage, but it is known and agreed that it works and works quickly. For something further to think about, there is also evidence that nutrients can be absorbed through the bark of trees. Spray away!

ORGANIC PEST CONTROL PRODUCTS

The following products and techniques are a guide for controlling insects with the least damage to Nature's balances. The organic pesticides that kill insects are better choices than the toxic chemicals, but I hope you only use them as a last resort since most of the pesticides can't tell the difference between a good bug and a bad one.

ANTIDESICCANTS: Also called antitranspirants, these products are made from pine oil and are nontoxic and biodegradable. They are sometimes used for the prevention of powdery mildew on roses and crape myrtles. They work by spreading a clear film over the leaves. They are also used to help control diseases. I'm a little concerned about how they gum up the surface of the leaves.

BACILLUS THURINGIENSIS (Bt): A beneficial bacteria applied as a spray to kill caterpillars. Sold under a variety of names such as Thuricide, Dipel, Bio-Worm, and others. Use *Bacillus thuringiensis* "Israelensis" (Bti) in water for the control of mosquito larvae. Use Garrett Juice with Bt for extra effect. Molasses also helps. It provides protein and keeps insect-killing bacteria alive on the foliage longer—even during rain. Bt "San Diego" is good for Colorado potato beetle, elm leaf beetle, and other leaf-chewing beetles.

BAKING SODA: Mixed at the rate of 4 teaspoons (1 rounded table-spoon) per gallon, baking soda makes an excellent fungicide for black spot, powdery mildew, brown patch, and other fungal problems. Be careful to keep the spray on the foliage and not on the soil as much as possible. Baking soda is composed of sodium and bicarbonate; both are necessary in the soil but only in very small amounts. Potassium bicarbonate is a better choice for the same use.

BLACK HOLE GOPHER TRAP: Guaranteed to trap your gophers, so the ad says. Gophers are notoriously hard to get rid of, and annoyingly destructive. Even if they don't wolf down your entire harvest-to-be, their tunnels and mounds can ruin your garden. The black hole trap works only on gophers and is safe around pets and children. Gophers live in round tunnels and have learned that square things (like most traps) are dangerous, so this trap is round, like the tunnels. When the trap is placed at the end of its tunnel, the gopher detects the air and light that the trap lets in. When it rushes to plug it up, a snare catches and kills it.

BORDEAUX MIX: A fungicide and insecticide usually made from copper sulfate and lime. Good for most foliar problems and an effective organic treatment for disease control on fruits, vegetables, shrubs, trees, and flowers such as anthracnose, botrytis blight, peach tree curl, and twig blight. Wet down decks and other hard surfaces before spraying, as some staining is possible. I do not recommend this product.

*Foliar feeding is an excellent way to give
plants fertilizer elements that are lacking in
the soil.*

CITRUS PRODUCTS: Orange, grapefruit and other citrus peelings can be frozen and later ground up into a pulp to serve as an effective rootknot nematode control. Mix the pulp into the soil at about 2–5 lbs./1,000 sq. ft. prior to planting crops tht are susceptable to the pests. The same material can be used as a fire ant control by tossing it around the mounds for the ants to forage.

To make an excellent cleaner for counters, walls, bathroom fixtures, etc., mix one ounce of orange or other citrus oil into one quart of water. This mix can also be used to kill indoor insect pests, but is too strong to spray plant foliage. To make your own homemade citrus oil, fill a container half full of any citrus peelings or pulp and the rest with water. Let sit for a week or so, strain the solids out and use 1–2 cups of your concentrate per gallon of spray. Commercial orange oil or d-limonene products are more powerful than the homemade versions. They are more powerful solvents and can burn plants. Use them at a rate of no more than 2 ounces per gallon of water as a pest control spray. For outdoor use, it is best to mix with molasses and compost tea.

COPPER: Trace mineral that in liquid form has been used as a fungal control. I no longer recommend it.

CONSAN 20: See Triple Action 20.

CORNMEAL: Disease control—Use cornmeal for root or soil borne fungus problems at 10–20 lbs./1,000 sq. ft. Cornmeal works as a disease fighter in the soil by providing and stimulating existing beneficial microorganisms that feed on pathogens such as rhizoctinia, better known as brown patch in St. Augustine. Cornmeal at about two lbs./100 sq. ft. also works on seedlings to prevents damping off, also on any other soil borne fungal diseases on both food and ornamental crops. One application may be all that is needed, but multiple applications are okay if necessary because cornmeal serves as a mild organic fertilizer and soil builder. The cornmeal needs moisture to activeate. Rain won't hurt conrmeal's efficacy because, like all organic products, it is not water soluble.

Algae Control—For floating paint-like and filamentous algae in water, use cornmeal at 5 lbs./1,000 sq. ft. or 150–200 lbs./surface acre. The cellulose in the cornmeal helps to tie up the excess phosphorous in water, balances the water chemistry and thus kills off the algae. The organic carbon in the cornmeal enables the beneficial bacteria in the water to flourish at the expense of the algae. Then the decomposing algae provide a source of carbon for the bacteria. One or two tratments is usually enough to control the algae for several months.

> Caution: Any fast algae kill from any product can cause an oxygen deprivation and result in fish kill.

Additional information can be obtained from the following publications:

"Cornmeal—it's not just hog feed anymore, *The Peanut Farmer*," May 1996.

Aquaculture Engineering 9 (1990) 175–186.

P.S. Cornmeal only works in an organic program. When toxic chemical products are used, the effect of the cornmeal will be lost.

DIATOMACEOUS EARTH (D.E.): Natural diatomaceous earth is approximately 5 percent aluminum, 5 percent sodium, 86 percent silicon. It is the skeletal remains of microscopic organisms (one celled aquatic plants called diatoms) that lived in sea water or freshwater lakes millions of years ago in the western United States. Apply using a dusting machine (manual or electrostatic) and cover plants or treatment area entirely. Be sure to use a dust mask when applying! DE is non-selective, so use sparingly. Breathing any dusty material can cause lung problems. As a food supplement, use at 1 to 2 percent of the food volume for feeding pets or livestock. Swimming pool DE has been partially melted and is much more dangerous to breathe. Use only natural diatomaceous earth that contains less than 1 percent crystalline silica dioxide.

> **Never use swimming pool DE for anything other than pool filters.**

DORMANT OIL: Long-standing, organic, winter treatment for scale and other over-wintering insects. Petroleum-based and will kill beneficial insects, so use sparingly. Spray dormant oil at temperatures between 40° and 80°. It works by smothering the over-wintering insects. Effective against scale, aphids, spider mites, and others. Do not use sulfur as a fungicide without waiting 30 days after using dormant oil. Horticultural oil is a much better choice.

FLOATING ROW-COVER: Gardening fabric designed to envelop plants in a moist, greenhouse warmth while allowing water, light, and ventilation for proper plant respiration. Protects foliage from chewing insects, prevents flies and moths from laying eggs, and reduces diseases carried by pests. Birds, rabbits, and other animals are discouraged from feeding on plants. On the other hand, it looks bad and gets in the way.

GARLIC/PEPPER TEA: An organic insect and disease control material made from the juice of garlic and hot peppers such as jalapeño, habanero, or cayenne. This is one of the few preventative controls that I recommend. It is effective for both ornamental and food crops.

LIME SULFUR: An organic fungicide (calcium polysulfide) for fruits, berries, roses, nuts, and ornamental plants. Spray plants as buds swell, but before they open. It is effective for powdery mildew, anthracnose, peach leaf curl, brown rot. Insects it controls include scale, mites and other insects. I do not recommend.

NICOTINE SULFATE: An old-time, organic pesticide used for the control of hard-to-kill insects. Although it is a quickly biodegradable product, it is extremely dangerous to handle and I do not recommend its use.

NOSEMA LOCUSTAE: A biological control for crickets and grasshoppers. It works the same way Bt works on caterpillars. It's applied as a dry bait, the insects eat the material, get sick, and are cannibalized by their friends. Charming, isn't it? But it works. Brand names include Nolo Bait, Grasshopper Attack, and Semispore.

OILS: There are now three types of spray oils: dormant, horticultural, and vegetable. Dormant oils are petroleum based, relatively free of impurities, and have been used as far back as 1880. Dormant oils have lower volatility and more insect-killing power than the other oils, but they can be more toxic to plants. These oils should only be used during the winter months when plants are dormant. Horticultural oils are the lightest and most pure petroleum oils. They can be used for spraying pecan trees and fruit trees, but they are also effective on shrubs and flowers that have scale or other insect infestations. Vegetable oils are plant extracts. They are environmentally safe, degrade quickly by evaporation, fit into organic or integrated pest management programs, are nonpoisonous to the applicator, are noncorrosive to the spray equipment, and kill a wide range of insects. The state of Texas is leaning toward vegetable oils. Drilling lubricants can no longer be petroleum oils.

POTASSIUM BICARBONATE: Natural fungal disease control. Can be purchased generically or as commercial fungicide. Use at a round table-spoon (4 teaspoons) per gallon of water. A much better choice than baking soda. Can be mixed with Garrett Juice or other organic sprays.

PYRETHRUM: Available in liquid or dry forms. Will kill a wide range of insects including aphids, beetles, leafhoppers, worms, caterpillars, and ants. It is short-lived and relatively nontoxic to animals. Pyrethrum is dried and powdered painted daisy (*Chrysanthemum cinerariaefolium*). Artificial chemical substitutes, called pyrethroids, should be avoided. Pyrethrin is the active ingredient in the natural product. Even though pyrethrum is a natural product, I no longer recommend it except as a last resort. There are less toxic alternatives.

ROTENONE: A botanical pesticide that can be used to kill aphids, worms, beetles, borers, and thrips. Strong solutions are effective on fire ants and hard-to-kill type beetles. No longer considered an acceptable organic product. Products available containing rotenone and pyrethroids are much too toxic. Safer alternatives exist that work as well or better. It is extremely dangerous to fish. I do not recommend.

RYANIA: Root extract from the ryania shrub, can be used as dust or spray to control moths, corn borer, and other problem insects. Ryania is a relatively strong organic pesticide. I don't recommend it. Safer alternatives exist.

SABADILLA: A botanical insecticide made from a tropical lily. It is effective on some of the hard-to-kill garden pests such as thrips, cabbage worms, grasshoppers, loopers, leafhoppers, harlequin bugs, adult squash, and cucumber beetles. This is a toxic organic product that I no longer recommend—which doesn't matter, since it isn't available anyway.

SOAP: Non-phosphate liquid soaps and water mixed together into a spray are used to control aphids and other small insects. Strong solutions can damage plant foliage, and even weak solutions can kill many of the microscopic beneficial insects and microorganisms, so use sparingly, if at all. There are better choices.

SULFUR: Finely ground sulfur is used by mixing with water or dusting on dry plants to control black spot, leaf spot, brown canker, rust, peach leaf curl, powdery mildew, apple scab, and many insect pests. Mix with liquid seaweed to enhance the fungicidal properties. Sulfur will also control fleas, mites, thrips, and chiggers. To avoid leaf burn, do not use when temperature is 90° or above. Sulfur will burn squash and other cucurbits such as pumpkins, gourds, and melons.

TANGLEFOOT: Spread on the bark of trees to control gypsy moths, canker worms, climbing cutworms, and ants. Made from natural gum resins, castor oil, and vegetable waxes. Old product that's useful in all organic programs. Do not put all the way around plant trunks—it will girdle the plants. Apply in strips or on a paper ring.

TRIPLE ACTION 20: Triple Action 20 is a synthetic fungicide but has extremely low toxicity and biodegrades very quickly. It offers good control of fireblight and other bacterial diseases. Use at 1 teaspoon per gallon. Also sold as Consan 20.

VINEGAR: Vinegar can be an effective tool for controlling a few problem fire ant mounds. Pour it directly into the center of the mound. Use the strongest dilution available. 5 percent and 10 percent vinegar are commonly available in the grocery store. Vinegar is an effective herbicide, so be careful to keep it off your good plants.

WEED FABRIC: Synthetic fabric that supposedly allows air and water movement, while at the same time blocking out some weed growth. For use in all gardening areas and under walkways, driveways, decks, and patios. I don't recommend it. Use a thick layer of mulch instead in order to maintain the natural processes in the soil.

YELLOW STICKY TRAPS: Nontoxic, bright-yellow cards that trap insects with their sticky coating. They are primarily used to monitor insect populations. They give some effective control in greenhouses, but not much.

COMPOST—MOTHER NATURE'S FERTILIZER

What is compost? How do you make a compost? Is compost a fertilizer? How do I use compost? Is composted manure in a bag really compost? Do I need bark, peat moss, and compost?

To answer all these questions, let's go through the entire composting process. For starters, everything on earth that's alive dies and everything that dies rots, and completely rotted material is compost. Yes, compost is a fertilizer. In fact, it is the best fertilizer, being Nature's own. Compost is not only an excellent fertilizer but also an excellent way to recycle waste. The word compost comes from two Latin words meaning "bring together."

The best composts are those that are made at home from several ingredients. The ideal mixture is about 80 percent vegetative matter and 20 percent animal waste. The best materials are those that you have on your own property. The second-best materials are those that can be easily gotten from near your property. The compost pile location can be in sun or shade, and covers are not necessary.

Even though there are many recipes for compost, it's almost impossible to foul up the compost-making process. For new gardens or planting beds, the composting can be done right on the ground by lightly tilling organic matter into the soil and mulching. To use this method effectively, it's best to do the work now and wait until next season to plant. Composting in the ground, as the forest does, simply takes longer than composting in a pile. Remember that composting is more of an art than

Compost—Mother Nature's Fertilizer

138

a science and a little experimenting is good. There are many acceptable ways to build compost piles, but I find that the simplest systems are usually the best.

The best time to compost is whenever the raw materials are available. It's ideal to have compost piles working year round. Choose a convenient site—some easily accessible, utility area such as behind the garage or in the dog run. The most effective compost piles are made on a paved surface so that the liquid leachate can be caught and used as a fertilizer. When the pile is on the ground, the leachate is wasted but the earthworms can enter the pile and help complete the natural degradation of the material.

Next, decide what kind of a container to use. I don't use a container at all but instead just pile the material on the ground or on a concrete slab. If you choose to use a container, buy some hog wire, lumber, wooden pallets, cinder blocks, or any materials that will hold a volume of about 4'x4' with a height of 3 feet. I would say a minimum compost pile should be 3'x3'x3'.

Hay or wheat-straw bales make an excellent container for compost. Build a two-or three-sided container by stacking the bales to make the sides. At the end of the composting process, the hay-bale sides can be pulled into the mix to become part of the compost. Wood containers will also rot and become part of the compost.

Many materials can be used to make compost. Some include grass clippings, leaves of all kinds, sawdust, spent plants, weeds (don't worry about the weed seed), tree chips, coffee grounds, feather meal, seaweed, peanut hulls, pecan hulls and other nut shells, fish scraps, brewery waste, slaughterhouse waste, paper, pine needles, wool, silk, cotton, granite dust, vegetable and meat scraps, fruit peelings and waste, pet hair, household dust, and animal manures. It's controversial whether dog and cat manure should be used in the compost pile. I don't have cats but I do use the dog manure. You should make your own decision on this point. I do not recommend using newspaper or other dyed or printed materials, synthetic fabrics, burned charcoal, plastics, or rubber.

What can be put in the compost pile?

Anything that was once alive.

The materials should be chopped into various-size pieces and thoroughly mixed together. Compost piles that contain nothing but one particle size will not breathe as well. Layering the ingredients, as most books recommend, is unnecessary unless it will help to get the proportions right. Remember that after the first turning the layers won't be there anymore. Also, remember that green plant material contains water and nitrogen and thus will break down faster than dry, withered materials. It's a good idea to add some native soil (a couple of shovels full) to each pile to inoculate the pile with native-soil microorganisms. To thrive, microorganisms need (1) an energy source, which is any carbon material such as leaves or wood, (2) a nitrogen source such as manure, green foliage, or organic fertilizers, (3) air, and (4) moisture.

Watering the pile thoroughly is important and best done while mixing the original ingredients together. The proper moisture level is between 40–50 percent, similar to the wetness of a squeezed-out sponge. Piles that are too wet will be anaerobic and not decay properly. Piles that are too dry won't compost properly or fast enough. Once you have gotten the pile evenly moist, it's easy to keep it there. Give it a little water during dry periods. If you have ants in your compost pile, it's too dry.

Turning the pile is important. Turning keeps the mixture aerobic by helping oxygen penetrate the material. Turning also ensures that all the ingredients are exposed to the beneficial fungi, bacteria, and other microorganisms that work to break the raw material down into humus. It also ensures that all the ingredients are exposed to the cleansing heat of the center of the pile. In a properly "cooking" compost pile, the heat of approximately 150° kills the weed seed and harmful pathogens but stimulates the beneficial microorganisms. Don't be concerned if your pile heats for a while and then cools off—that's natural. The entire process takes anywhere from two months to a year depending on how often the pile is turned. If the ingredients contain a high percentage of wood chips, the process may take even longer. It's interesting that softwood sawdust and chips break down more slowly than hardwood.

Compost activators can be helpful in getting the pile to heat up and cook faster. Although most any organic fertilizer can be used as a compost activator, they should be mixed into the pile at 3–4 lbs./cubic yard of compost. Molasses can also help.

Compost can be used in many ways. Partially completed compost makes a very effective topdressing mulch for ornamental or vegetable gardens. It's easy to tell when the compost is finished and ready to use as a fertilizer and soil amendment. The original material will no longer be identifiable, the texture will be soft and crumbly, and the fragrance will be rich and earthy.

Compost can be used to fertilize grass areas, planting beds, vegetable gardens, and potted plants. It is the only organic material I recommend for the preparation of new planting beds. Why is compost better than pine bark or peat moss? Because it's alive, and those other materials are not.

APPENDIX

Edible & Medicinal Landscaping Plants

(These are all herbs—not 'erbs!)

SHADE TREES:
Ginkgo—tea from leaves
Jujube—fruit
Linden—tea from flowers
Mulberry—fruit
Pecan—edible nuts
Persimmon—fruit
Walnut—edible nuts

SHRUBS:
Agarita—fruit for wine
Althea—edible flowers
Bay—tea and food seasoning from leaves
Germander—freshens air indoors
Pomegranate—edible fruit
Turk's cap—flowers and fruit for tea

ANNUALS:
Begonias—edible flowers
Daylilies—edible flowers
Dianthus—edible flowers
Ginger—food seasoning and tea from roots
Hibiscus—edible flowers
Johnny jump-ups—edible flowers
Nasturtium—edible leaves
Pansies—edible flowers
Peanuts—edible nuts
Purslane—edible leaves
Sunflower—edible seeds and flower petals

VINES:
Beans and Peas—edible pods and seed
Gourds—dippers and bird houses
Grapes—food fruit and leaves
Luffa—sponges from the fruit, edible flowers
Malabar spinach—edible foliage
Passion flower—edible fruit, tea from leaves

ORNAMENTAL TREES:
Apple—fruit and edible flower petals
Apricot—fruit and edible flower petals
Citrus—edible fruit
Crabapple—fruit and edible flower petals
Fig—fruit and edible flower petals
Mexican plum—fruit
Peach—fruit and edible flower petals
Pear—fruit and edible flower petals
Persimmon—fruit
Plum—fruit and edible flower petals
Redbud—edible flowers
Rusty blackhaw viburnum—edible berries
Witchhazel—tea from leaves

PERENNIALS:
Anise hyssop—edible flowers, foliage for tea
Blackberries—edible berries, foliage for tea
Chives—edible foliage and flowers
Garlic—edible flowers, greens, and cloves
Hibiscus—edible flowers
Hoja santa—leaves for cooking with meats
Horsemint—insect repellent
Jerusalem artichoke—edible roots
Lavender—teas and insect repellent
Monarda—edible flowers and leaves for teas
Peppers—edible fruit
Purple coneflower—all plant parts for teas
Rosemary—edible flowers, foliage for teas
Roses—petals and hips for tea
Salvia—edible flowers, foliage for teas
Sweet marigold—food flavoring and tea from leaves and flowers
Tansy—chopped and crushed foliage repels ants
Turk's cap—flowers & fruit for tea

GROUND COVERS:

Clover—tea from leaves and flowers
Creeping thyme—teas and food flavoring
Gotu kola—tea from leaves
Mints—food and teas from flowers and leaves
Oregano—teas and food flavoring
Violets—leaves in salads and tea from flowers and leaves

Note: Pregnant women should avoid all strong herbs and no plant should be ingested in excess by anyone. None of these should be eaten unless they are being grown organically.

EDIBLE FLOWERS

Aloe vera, althea, apple blossoms, arugula, basil, begonia, borage, broccoli, calendula, chicory, chives (onion and garlic), clover, coriander, dandelion, dill, elderberry, English daisy, fennel, hyssop lavender, lemon, lilac, mint, monarda (red flowered *M. didyma*), mum (base of petal is bitter), mustard, okra, orange, oregano, pea (except for sweet peas), pineapple sage, radish, redbud, rosemary, scented geranium, society garlic, sweet woodruff, squash blossoms, thyme, violet, winter savory, yucca (petals only).

RULES FOR EDIBLE FLOWERS

1 Not all flowers are edible. Some are poisonous. Learn the difference.

2 Eat flowers only when you are positive they are edible and nontoxic.

3 Eat only flowers that have been grown organically,.

4 Do not eat flowers from florists, nurseries, or garden centers unless you know they've been maintained organically.

5 Do not eat flowers if you have hay fever, asthma, or allergies.

6 Do not eat flowers growing on the side of the road.

7 Remove pistils and stamens from flowers before eating. Eat only the petals, especially of large flowers.

8 Introduce flowers into your diet the way you would new foods to a baby—one at a time in small quantities.

SICK TREE TREATMENT

Oak wilt is one of the most serious tree problems in Texas. It is a devastating disease of native and introduced red oaks and live oaks. The Texas Forest Service has been working on the problem for several years and recommends a program of trenching to separate the roots of sick trees from those of healthy trees and injection of a chemical fungicide called Alamo. I don't recommend this program and have a different proposal.

To look at this problem from a little bit different angle, let's consider the insect that's blamed. The nitidulid or sap-feeding beetle, the alleged culprit, feeds on tree sap in the spring and spreads the disease. Adult beetles look like tiny June bugs. They inhabit the fungal mats beneath the bark of diseased red oaks (*Quercus texana* and *Quercus shumardii*). Infectious beetles emerge from the fungal mats and deposit oak wilt spores in wounds on healthy trees by feeding on sap. These are the same insects that feed on rotting fruit in the orchard.

There is research evidence now that sapsuckers (a beautiful but, unfortunately, destructive bird) attack and drill holes in trees that are in stress. The stress causes sweeter and more concentrated sugars. The sap beetles are probably attracted to trees in a similar way. But even if the little beetles go to both healthy and weak trees, why do some trees succumb to the disease and some don't? Even if the beetles don't infect every tree, the roots reach far out and touch the surrounding tree roots. All the experts agree that the disease can easily spread through the roots. Even though the oak wilt disease has killed thousands of live oaks and red oaks in Texas, the disease can be stopped by using organic techniques. The plan is simple. Keep trees in a healthy condition so their immune system can resist the infection and disease. It has been noticed by many farmers and ranchers that the disease doesn't bother some tree— especially those that are mulched and those where the natural habitat under trees has been maintained.

There's only experimental evidence so far but we have seen excellent results from the following organic program:

Aerate the root zone heavily. Start between the dripline and the trunk and go far out beyond the dripline. A 7–12" depth of the aeration holes is ideal but any depth is beneficial. An alternative is to spray the root zone with a microbe product such as Bio-Innoculant.

Apply Texas greensand at about 80 lbs. per 1,000 sq. ft., lava sand at about 80 lbs./1,000 sq. ft., cornmeal at about 20 lbs./1,000 sq. ft. and sugar or dry molasses at about 5 lbs./1,000 sq. ft. Cornmeal is a natural disease fighter and sugar is a carbon source to feed the microbes in the soil.

Apply a 1" layer of compost followed by a 3–5" layer of shredded native tree trimmings. Native cedar is the very best source for mulch.

Spray the foliage monthly or more often if possible with Garrett Juice (see formula below). For large-scale farms and ranches, a one-time spraying is beneficial if the budget doesn't allow ongoing sprays. Adding garlic tea to the spray is also beneficial while the tree is in trouble.

Stop using high nitrogen fertilizers and toxic chemical pesticides. The pesticides kill the beneficial nematodes and insects. The fake fertilizers are destructive to the important micorrhizal fungi on the roots.

A premix of lava, greensand, and compost is now available from the organic suppliers. All you'll have to add is cornmeal and topdressing mulch.

Since the fungal mats form on red oaks only, not on live oaks, the live oak wood can be used for firewood without any worry of spreading the oak wilt disease. Red oak wood needs to be stacked in a sunny location and covered with clear plastic to form a greenhouse effect to kill the beetles and fungal mats. When oaks are shredded into mulch, the aeration kills the pathogens and eliminates the possibility of disease spread. That goes for all species.

Is this beetle the only way the problem could be spread? I doubt it. How about mechanical damage to tree trunks, wind, squirrels, hail, sapsuckers and other insects? Fire ants seem to prefer weaker trees over others and could be part of the spreading problem.

My recommended program has not yet been proven by any university and probably won't be, even though the evidence continues to stack up. Improving the health of the soil and thus the population of beneficial fungi on the root system seems to be paramount. Spraying the foliage during the rebuilding of the soil and root system provides trace minerals into the plant that can't yet come in through the roots. This program is not just for oak wilt. It works for most environmental tree problems and all tree types. My point here is that if it works for oak wilt, it will work even more effectively for less deadly tree conditions. If your tree problem is a result of poor variety selection, I can only help you in the future. Choose more wisely next time.

For any physical damage to trunks, spray with hydrogen peroxide and then treat wounds with Tree Trunk Goop (see recipe below).

Tree Trunk Goop

⅓ manure compost   ⅓ soft rock phosphate
⅓ natural diatomaceous earth (DE)

Add enough water to make a wet paste and slather on tree wounds.
Replace if it is washed off by rain or irrigation.

CONVERSION TABLES

CHEMICAL MIXING CHART AND RECIPES

Use this table to determine the amount of liquid/dry chemicals to add to water based on a standard of a given amount per 100 gallons in the manufacturer's instructions. Example: If the manufacturer recommends 8 oz. per 100 gallons, and 1 gallon of mix is required, read the table from left to right, 8 oz./100 gallon column over to ½ tsp./gallon column.

CHEMICAL MIXING CHART AND RECIPES

Liquid Equivalent Table

100 gal	25 gal	12½ gal	5 gal	1 gal
2 gal	2 qt	1 qt	12¾ oz	2½ oz.
1 gal	1 qt	1 pt	6½ oz	2½ tbs.
2 qts	1 pt	8 oz	3¼ oz	3¾ tsp.
3 pt	12 oz	6 oz	5 tbs.	1 tbs.
1 qt	½ pt	4 oz	3 tbs.	2 tsp.
1½ pt	6 oz	3 oz	2½ tbs.	1½ tsp.
1 pt	4 oz	2 oz	5 tsp.	1 tsp.
8 oz	2 oz	1 oz	3 tsp.	½ tsp.

Powder (Dry) Equivalent Table

100 gal	25 gal	12½ gal	5 gal	1 gal
5 lb	1¼ lb	12 oz	4 oz	4 ⅘ tsp.
4 lb	1 lb	8 oz	3½ oz	3 ⅘ tsp.
3 lb	12 oz	6 oz	2⅜ oz	2 ⅘ tsp
2 lb	8 oz	4 oz	1¾ oz	2 tsp
1 lb	4 oz	2 oz	⅞ oz	1 tsp
8 oz	2 oz	1 oz	⅜ oz	½ tsp.
4 oz	1 oz	½ oz	3/16 oz	¼ tsp.

1 oz. = 6 tsp. (liq.), 9 tsp. (dry); 1 oz. = 2 tbs. (liq.), 5 tbs. (dry); 1 tbs. = 3 tsp. (liq), 4 tsp. (dry)

APPLICATION RATE CHART

800 lbs./acre = 20 lbs./1,000 sq. ft.
400 lbs./acre = 10 lbs./1,000 sq. ft.
250 lbs./acre = 6 lbs./1,000 sq. ft.
200 lbs./acre = 5 lbs./1,000 sq. ft.
1 qt./acre = 2 tbs./1,000 sq. ft. = 1 oz./1,000 sq. ft.
13 oz./acre = 1 tsp./1,000 sq. ft. = 3 oz./1,000 sq. ft.
11 gal./acre = 1 qt./1,000 sq. ft.
1 qt./acre = 2 tbs./1,000 sq. ft.
1 lb./acre = .4 oz./1,000 sq. ft.
1.5 oz./acre = 7 drops/gal./1,000 sq. ft.
13 oz./acre = 1 tsp./1,000 sq. ft.
4 oz./acre = .10 oz./1,000 sq. ft. (30 drops per gal.)
8 oz./acre = .20 oz./1,000 sq. ft. (60 drops per gal.)
1 ton/acre = 4.6 lb. per 100 sq. ft. = .4 lb. per sq. yd.

Appendix

APPLICATION RATE CHART (continued)

3 tons/acre = 14 lb. per 100 sq. ft. = 1.25 lb. per sq. yd.
10 tons/acre = 46 lb. per 100 sq. ft. = 4 lb. per sq. yd.
1 gal./10 acres = 13 oz./acre
1.5 gal./10 acres = 19 oz./acre
.5 gal./10 acres = 6 oz./acre
6" soil = 2 million lbs./acre

LINEAR MEASURE

1 foot	12 inches		
1 hand	$\frac{1}{3}$ foot	4 inches	
1 span	9 inches		
1 yard	3 feet		
1 rod	16$\frac{1}{2}$ feet	5$\frac{1}{2}$ yards	
1 furlong	40 poles	220 yards	
1 mile	8 furlongs	5,200 feet	320 rods
1 league	3 miles		
1 degree	69$\frac{1}{8}$ miles		

SQUARE OR AREA MEASURE

1 square foot	144 square inches	
1 square yard	9 square feet	
1 acre	160 square rods	43,560 sq. ft.
1 section	640 acres	1 square mile
1 hectare	2.47 acres	

COMMON MEASUREMENTS

One pinch/dash	$\frac{1}{16}$ tsp.
1 ounce	360 drops
1 teaspoon	$\frac{1}{6}$ ounce (60 drops)
1 tablespoon	3 tsp. ($\frac{1}{2}$ oz. liquid, 180 drops)
1 gallon (gal.)	769 tsp. (256 tbs., 128 oz., 32 cups, 16 pints, 4 qts.)
4 tablespoons	$\frac{1}{4}$ cup (2 ounces liquid)
$\frac{1}{3}$ cup	5 tablespoons plus 1 teaspoon
$\frac{1}{2}$ cup	8 tablespoons (4 ounces liquid)
1 gill	$\frac{1}{2}$ cup (4 ounces liquid)
1 cup	16 tablespoons (8 ounces liquid)
1 pint (pt.)	2 cups (16 ounces liquid)
1 quart (qt.)	2 pints (32 ounces liquid)
4 quarts	1 gallon
1 peck	8 quarts
1 bushel	4 pecks
1 pound	16 ounces (dry measure)
1 barrel (bbl.)	31$\frac{1}{2}$ gallons
1 acre foot	325,000 gallons

CUBIC OR VOLUME MEASURE

1 cubic foot	1,728 cubic inches
1 cubic yard	27 cubic feet
2 cord of wood	128 cubic feet

(A legal cord of wood is 4 feet high, 4 feet wide, and 8 feet long.)

1 board foot	144 cubic inches	$\frac{1}{12}$ cubic foot

METRIC EQUIVALENTS

Linear

1 millimeter (mm.)	.0394 in.	
1 centimeter (cm.)	.3937 in.	
1 decimeter (dm.)	3.937 in.	
1 meter (m.)	39.37 in.	1.1 yard
1 decameter	393.7 in.	10 yd. 2.8 ft.
1 hectometer	328 ft. 1 in.	
1 kilometer	3,280 ft. 1 in.	

CONVERSIONS

1 sq. yd.	9 sq. ft.
1 cu. yd.	27 cu. ft.

DRY MEASURE

1 quart	2 pints
1 peck	8 quarts
1 bushel (bu.)	4 pecks

COMMON EQUIVALENTS

1 bushel	2,150 cubic inches or 1 ¼ cubic ft.
1 gallon	231 cubic inches
1 cubic foot	7½ gallons
1 cubic foot of water	62½ pounds (62.43 lb.)
1 gallon of water	8⅓ pounds (8.345 lb.)
1 cubic foot of ice	57½ pounds

APPLICATIONS RATES (BULK MATERIAL)

(1 cu. ft.=)	(1 cu. yd.=)	(3 cu.ft. bagged)	(2 cu. ft. bagged)
12 sq. ft. 1" deep	1,296 sq. ft. ¼" deep	36 sq. ft. 1" deep	96 sq.ft. ¼" deep
6 sq. ft. 2" deep	648 sq. ft. 1/2" deep	18 sq. ft. 2" deep	48 sq.ft. ½" deep
4 sq. ft. 3" deep	324 sq. ft. I" deep	12 sq. ft. 3" deep	24 sq.ft. 1" deep
3 sq. ft. 4" deep	162 sq. ft. 2" deep	9 sq. ft. 4" deep	12 sq.ft. 2" deep
	108 sq. ft. 3" deep		8 sq.ft. 3" deep
	81 sq. ft. 4" deep		6 sq.ft. 4" deep

CONVERSION TABLES

U.S.		Abbreviations	Metric		
1 teaspoon	60 drops	Teaspoon	t.	1 teaspoon	5 milliliters
1 tablespoon	3 teaspoons	Tablespoon	T.	1 tablespoon	15 milliliters
1 tablespoon	180 drops	Cup	c.	1 ounce	30 milliliters
1 ounce	2 tablespoons	Pint	pt.	1 quart	.940 liters
1 ounce	360 drops	Quart	qt.	1 gallon	3.76 liters
1 cup	8 ounces	Gallon	gal.		
1 pound	16 ounces	Ounce	oz.		
1 pint (16 oz.)	2 cups	Pound	lb.		
1 quart (32 oz.)	2 pints	Milliliter	ml.		
1 gallon (128oz.)	4 quarts	Liter	l.		
1 gallon	16 cups				
1 gallon	128 ounces				

DILUTION CHART (Gallons of Water)

Dilution	1 Qt.	1 Gal.	3 Gal.	5 Gal.	10 Gal.	15 Gal.
1–10	3 oz.	12 oz.	2¼ pts.	2 qts.	3¾ qts.	5½ qts.
1–50	4 t.	5 T.	7½ oz.	12½ oz.	25 oz.	37½ oz.
1–80	1 T.	2 oz.	6 oz.	10 oz.	20 oz.	30 oz.
1–100	2 t.	2½ T.	3½ oz.	6¼ oz.	12½ oz.	19 oz.
1–200	1 t.	4 t.	2 oz.	3½ oz.	6½ oz.	10 oz.
1–400	½ t.	2 t.	2 T.	1½ oz.	3 oz.	5 oz.
1–800	—	1 t.	1 T.	5 t.	1½ oz.	2½ oz.

SOIL NUTRIENT AVAILABILITY

Nutrient	Low	Normal	High	Very High
Calcium	<20 percent	20–60	60–80	>80
Magnesium	<10 percent	10–25	25–35	>35
Potassium	<5 percent	5–20	20–30	>30
Phosphorus	<.1 percent	.1–.4	.5–.8	>.8
Nitrogen	<1 ppm	1–10	10–20	>20
Nitrate	<5 ppm	5–50	50–100	>100
Sulfate	<30 ppm	30–90	90–180	>180
Sulfur	<10 ppm	10–30	30–60	>60

ppm represents parts per million
Percentage represents available percentages in the soil.

PRODUCT RATE CHART

Product	Rate	Frequency/Comments
Alfalfa meal	20 to 25 lbs. per 1,000 sq. ft.	Once a year in conjunction with other organic fertilizers.
Alliance Soil Ammendment	20 to 100 lbs. per 1,000 sq. ft.	Add to new bed preparations and as a subtly powerful organic fertilizer.
Bat guano	10 to 20 lbs. per 1,000 sq. ft.	Once a year to flowering plants or at each flower rotation.
Blood meal	10 to 20 lbs. per 1,000 sq. ft.	May be combined with cottonseed meal (4 parts cottonseed meal to 1 part blood meal).
Bone meal	110 to 210 lbs. per 1,000 sq. ft.	Once a year when planting bulbs or flowers. Watch for calcium buildup.
Cow manure	20 to 30 lbs. per 1,000 sq. ft. up to 5 tons per acre	Use composted manure to avoid weeds; raw material good to use on agricultural fields. Watch for buildup of phosphates and nitrates.
Cottonseed meal	20 to 30 lbs. per 1,000 sq. ft.	Use once or twice a year. May be combined with blood meal or other meals.
Colloidal phosphate	25 to 50 lbs. per 1,000 sq. ft.	Use once per year to give a long-lasting source of phosphorus and calcium. Put small handful into planting hole of new plants.
Compost	¼-inch depth on lawns; 2-inch depth in beds. 900–1,200 lbs./ac. on agriculture fields	Once a year to lawns and planting beds is ideal. Not important if beds are mulched.
Earthworm castings	10 lbs. per 1,000 sq. ft.	Use once per year or at each annual flower rotation on flowering plants as a supplemental food. Put a small handful in each planting hole.
Epsom salts	1 tbs. per gal.	Spray monthly if needed. Can be mixed with other sprays. For soils deficient in sulfur and magnesium.
Fish emulsion	2 oz./gal of water per 1,000 sq. ft.	Spray all plants 2 to 3 times per year or any time extra greening or pest control is needed.

Product Rate Chart, Continued

Product	Rate	Frequency/Comments
Fish meal	20 lbs. per 1,000 sq. ft.	Once or twice a year to lawns or planting beds as a supplemental fertilizer. Use 10 pounds per 1,000 sq. ft. after the first year.
Granite sand	10 lbs. per 1,000 sq. ft. up to 5 tons per acre.	Once a year as a mineral supplement. Can also be used to top-dress new, solid-sod installations.
Greensand	10 to 20 lbs. per 1,000 sq. ft.	Excellent mineral supplement.
Humate (Dry)	5–10 lbs. per 1,000 sq. ft.	Use high quality humate (40–50 percent, humic acid) at 50 lbs./acre once per year.
Humate (Liquid)	1–2 oz. per 1,000 sq. ft.	Spray all foliage lightly 3 times per growing season. Can be mixed with other liquid products.
Hydrogen peroxide (H_2O_2)	1 oz of 35 percent material per gal./1,000 sq. ft. or 8 oz. of 3 percent material per gal. per 1,000 sq. ft.	Can be mixed with other materials but always add the H_2O_2 first.
Lava sand	10 lbs. per 1,000 sq. ft. up to 5 tons per acre	Once a year as a mineral supplement. Can also be used to topdress new solid sod installations.
Manalfa	800 lbs./acre or 20 lbs. per 1,000 sq. ft.	10 lbs./1,000 sq. ft. after 1st full year.
Manure on fields	500–1,000 lbs./acre	In the beginning, as much as 5 tons per acre can be used until fertility levels increase.
Molasses	1 oz. per gal. of water or other liquids dry-20 lbs./1,000 sq. ft.	Apply as a foliar and soil spray to fertilize and feed microbes.
Molasses (dry)	5–10 lbs. per 1,000 sq. ft.	Apply to soil that is not yet healthy. One application a year is usually enough.
Organic fertilizers in general	20 lbs./1,000 sq. ft.	½ tsp./4" pot, 1 tsp./gal, 1 tbs./5 gal. container. Water in after application.
Poultry manure	20 lbs. per 1,000 sq. ft. the first year; 10 pounds thereafter. Composted only	Apply twice per year as a good natural source of nitrogen.

Product Rate Chart, Continued

Product	Rate	Frequency/Comments
Seaweed (Liquid kelp)	½ to 1 oz. per 1,000 sq. ft.	Apply to lawns and planting beds once a month as a supplement between applications of dry fertilizers.
Seaweed (Kelp meal)	10 to 20 lbs./l,000 sq. ft.	Apply to lawns and planting beds once a month as a supplement between applications of dry fertilizers.
Seaweed and Fish emulsion	Mix 1 oz. of seaweed and 2 oz. of fish emulsion per gallon of water	Apply as a general foliar spray to aid insect and fungus control and as a foliar feed. Spray all plants and lawns.
Soybean meal	20 lbs. per 1,000 sq. ft.	Apply twice per year.
Sul-Po-Mag	20 lbs. per 1,000 sq. ft.	Use once per year on soil needing sulfur, magnesium, and potassium.
Vinegar	½ oz. per gal.	Mix with other liquid products use 1 to 2 gal. of mix per 1,000 sq. ft.
Volcanite	20–40 lbs. per 1,000 sq. ft.	Apply as needed to add trace minerals and to increase soil paramagnetism.

HOMEMADE FORMULAS

PHARAOH ANT BAIT
(Sugar Ants)
1 teaspoon of creamy peanut butter
1 pat of butter or oleo
1 tablespoon of any light syrup
1 teaspoon of boric acid powder

Blend the above ingredients over low heat until smooth—be careful not to burn the solution. Put the finished bait into lids or other small containers. The ants will find them. This amount will make several bait stations. Feed ants as long as they will take the bait. Do not use this recipe on your waffles or pancakes. Remember that boric acid is poison. Change the sweet ingredients from time to time to prevent the ants from catching on.

Dust baking soda in problem areas.

Homemade Formulas (continued)

ROACH BAITS

An even less toxic bait can be made by mixing Arm and Hammer detergent together in a 50–50 mix with sugar.

To make boric balls, mix 1 teaspoon boric acid, 1 cup flour, ½ cup sugar and water. Roll into cakes and place behind appliances out of the reach of pets and children.

Note: Remember, D.E. (diatomaceous earth) for pets and pests is not the same as swimming pool D.E. Buy D.E. only from your local organic retailer.

GARLIC/PEPPER TEA INSECTICIDE

Liquefy 2 bulbs of garlic and 2 hot peppers in a blender ⅓ full of water. Strain the solids and add enough water to the garlic/pepper juice to make 1 gallon of concentrate. Use ¼ cup of concentrate per gallon of spray. For added strength, add 2 ounces of citrus oil for each gallon of water in the sprayer. To make garlic tea, omit the pepper and add another bulb of garlic.

BAKING SODA FUNGICIDE

Mix 4 teaspoons (about 1 rounded tablespoon) of baking soda and 1 teaspoon of liquid soap or vegetable oil into one gallon of water. Spray lightly on foliage of plants afflicted with black spot, powdery mildew, brown patch, and other fungal diseases. Avoid overusing, and try to keep out of the soil. Do not mix baking soda with other sprays. Potassium bicarbonate is even better than baking soda.

VINEGAR FUNGICIDE

Mix 3 tablespoons of natural apple cider vinegar in one gallon of water. Spray during the cool part of the day for black spot on roses and other fungal diseases. Mix with Garrett Juice for even more power.

COMPOST TEA

Compost tea is effective on many pests because of certain microorganisms that exist in it naturally and because of others that it stimulates. Fill the 5–15 gallon bucket half full of compost and finish filling with water. Let the mix sit for 10–14 days and then dilute and spray on the foliage of any and all plants including fruit trees, perennials, annuals, vegetables, roses, and other plants. It's effective on black spots on roses and early blight on tomatoes. How to dilute the dark compost tea before using depends on the compost used. A rule of thumb is to dilute the leachate down to one part compost liquid to four to ten parts water. It should look like iced tea. Be sure to strain the solids out with old pantyhose, cheese cloth or row floating cover material. Malcolm Beck says fill the container full of compost, slowly add water, and use anytime after 36 hours.

GARRETT JUICE
You can buy Garden-Ville Garrett Juice commercially or you can make your own. Per gallon of water: 1 cup manure compost tea, 1 ounce molasses, 1 ounce natural apple cider vinegar, 1 ounce liquid seaweed. For added disease control: ¼ cup garlic tea.

TREE TRUNK GOOP
⅓ part of each of the following mixed in enough water to make a wet paste: soft rock phosphate, natural diatomaceous earth, manure compost. Slop it on the trunk. Note: Fireplace ashes can be substituted for the soft rock phosphate.

GARDEN-VILLE FIRE ANT CONTROL
Equal parts compost tea or liquid humate, molasses, and orange oil. Mix 4–6 ounces per gallon of water to drench fire ant mounds. Use only 2–4 ounces per gallon for spraying plants for insect pests.

Note: Never store homemade brews in glass or any tightly sealed container.

GARLIC FLY KILLER
Recycle the pulp from the garlic tea preparation by adding some water to solids and set it outside, several feet from the back door. It not only attracts flies but kills them in the process. Later, toss it in the compost pile.

REPELLENT FOR PETS, RABBITS, AND SQUIRRELS
Dog-B-Gone—1 part cayenne pepper, 1 part dry mustard powder, 2 parts flour. Sprinkle on top of ground. Don't water in! Rover will quit going there eventually and mark other territory, and you will no longer need to treat original area. Will need to re-treat if there is rain. Cayenne pepper by itself usually works. Habanero works even better.

FLEA BATH
For fleas in the house, use a camera tripod to hang a 40-watt light bulb directly over a pan of soapy water. The fleas go for the light, end up in the soapy water, and drown.

INTERIOR ANT CONTROL
Crushed or chopped pieces of tansy leaf or bay leaf will repel ants quite effectively. A light dusting of cinnamon is also very effective.

BEER TRAPS
For slug, snail, and pill bug infestations, pour a small amount of cheap, stale beer (drink the good, cold beer) into a small dish or buried plastic cup. Clean out daily and refill as long as problem persists. A tablespoon of brewer's yeast in water also works.

Note: Keep insecticides away from children and pets. Don't breathe the dust of any dusty products. And remember that anything chemical or organic can injure or can kill if mishandled—there is no such thing as nontoxic!

RESOURCES

PUBLICATIONS

Acres U.S.A., a monthly publication on eco-agriculture. P.O. Box 91299, Austin, TX 78709, 1-800-355-5313.

Agriculture Testament and *Soil Health* by Sir Alfred Howard are state-of-the-art guides to organics and the use of compost to bring soil back to health. They were written in the 1940s, but are still two of the best publications on the market. Oxford and Rodale Press.

The Albrecht Papers by William Albrecht is a compilation of papers by the late Dr. Albrecht and is considered the bible for managing soil health. Published by Acres U.S.A.

Bread from Stones by Julius Hensel is a classic explaining the role of earth minerals in the production of wholesome food crops. Acres U.S.A.

Common Sense Pest Control by William Olkowski, Sheila Daar, Helga Olkowski is an excellent reference for low-toxicity pest control. The Taunton Press.

The Dirt Doctor's Guide to Organic Gardening by J. Howard Garrett is a compilation of essays covering all aspects of organic gardening from bed preparation to making herb tea. University of Texas Press.

Edible and Useful Plants of Texas and the Southwest by Delena Tull focuses on how to identify and use plants that grow in Texas and surrounding regions of the South and Southwest. University of Texas Press.

Appendix

Establishment and Maintenance of Landscape Plants by Dr. Carl Whitcomb provides excellent research and backup for the practical approach to horticulture. Lacebark Publications.

The Garden-Ville Method (Lessons in Nature) is written by the king of compost, Malcolm Beck, one of the most knowledgeable people on organics in the country. Malcolm Beck, 7561 E. Evans Road, San Antonio, TX 78266, 210-651-6115.

Growing Great Garlic, Ron Engeland, Acres U.S.A., 800-355-5313.

Holistic Resource Management by Alan Savory is a book for anyone involved in the management of land. This book teaches you how to think and to treat people and their environments as one whole. Island Press, Washington, DC.

Howard Garrett's Texas Organic Gardening provides organic information specifically for Texas, including plant varieties, planting instructions, and maintenance techniques. Houston: Gulf Publishing Company, 1993.

How to Have a Green Thumb Without an Aching Back, Exposition Press, *Gardening Without Work*, Devin-Adair, and *The No Work Gardening Book*, Rodale Press, by Ruth Stout are great. She was a humorous writer, a philosopher, and an advocate of mulching.

Landscape Design . . . Texas Style by Howard Garrett. This book is a well-kept secret about my design and landscape philosophy as well as a rather decent reference book on landscape construction and regional plant material selection. Out of print but can be found in libraries.

Mother Nature's Herbal by Judy Griffin, Ph.D. Llewellyn Publications, St. Paul, MN.

Nature's Silent Music by Dr. Phil Callahan explains how to preserve the health of the land by avoiding toxic chemicals and working within Nature's laws and systems. Acres U.S.A.

The One-Straw Revolution by Masanobu Fukuoka is an introduction to natural farming and an excellent book on the philosophy and practicality of organic gardening from one of Japan's living legends.

Organic Method Primer Basics by Bargyla Rateaver not only explains how plants absorb chunks of materials, including whole bacteria, they have electron microscope photos of the process in action. Books are available direct from 9049 Covina St., San Diego, CA 92126. Send a check for $25.00 for the Organic Method Primer Basics or $200.00 for the update. The prices cover taxes and shipping.

Plants of the Metroplex by Howard Garrett is totally revised and covers the trees, shrubs, ground covers, vines, and flowers that do well and those that don't do well. University of Texas Press.

Seaweed and Plant Growth by Dr. T. L. Senn explains in detail the wonderful powers of seaweed as a fertilizer, growth stimulator, and pest repellent.

The Secret Life of Compost by Malcolm Beck is a "how to" and "why" guide to composting. Acres U.S.A.

Science in Agriculture by Dr. Arden Anderson is a "must-have" and "must-study" book for anyone interested in eco-agriculture. Acres U.S.A.

Silent Spring by Rachel Carson is a must-read. If you don't convert to organics after reading this classic, you never will. The Riverside Press, Cambridge.

Texas Bug Book by Howard Garrett and Malcolm Beck is a complete review of the beneficial and pest insects of Texas. University of Texas Press.

Texas Organic Vegetable Gardening Book by Howard Garrett and Malcolm Beck is the only organic book on the vegetables, fruit and edible landscape plants for Texas. Gulf Publishing Co.

The Three Sisters: Exploring an Iroquois Garden is a Cornell Cooperative Extension publication. Requests should be sent to Cornell University, Media Services Resource Center, 7 BTP, Ithaca, NY 14850.

Weeds by Charles Walters is a thorough review and explanation of how to control weeds through soil management. Acres U.S.A.

ORGANIC GROWERS AND SUPPLIERS

Garden-Ville—(Organic products)—210-651-6115, 7561 E. Evans Road, San Antonio, TX 78266.

Green Mama's—(Organic products) 817-514-7336, 5324 Davis Blvd., N. Richland Hills, TX 76180.

Integrated Pest Management— 818-287-1101, 305 Agostino Road, San Gabriel, CA 91776.

Marshall Distributing Company—(Organic products, books, and animal supplies). 800-658-5699, 2224 E. Lancaster, Ft. Worth, TX 76103.

M&R Durango—(Beneficial insects) 800–526–4075, P.O. Box 886, Bayfield, CO 81122.

Muenster Milling Company—(Natural animal foods) 800-772-7178, 202 South Main, Muenster, TX 76252.

Native American Seed Co.— (Buffalograss and wildflower seed) Mail Order Station, 127 N. 16th St., Junction, TX 76849, 800-728-4043 www.seedsource.com

Natural Gardening Research Center—(Organic products) 812-623-3800, P.O. Box 149, Sunman, IN 47041.

OrCon, Inc.—(Beneficial insects) 213-937-7444, 5132 Venice Blvd., Los Angeles, CA 90019.

Organic Pest Management—(Beneficial insects) 206-367-0707, P.O. Box 55267, Seattle, WA 98155.

Peaceful Valley Farm Supply— 916-265-3276, 1173 Peaceful Valley Rd., Nevada City, CA 95959. Mail order pest controls, organic fertilizers, nursery stock, seeds, tools, and consulting.

Redenta's Garden—(Organic products) 817-451-2149, 5111 W. Arkansas Lane, Arlington, TX 76016 (corporate office).

Rincon-Vitova Insectaries—(Beneficial insects) 800-248-BUGS, P.O. Box 1555, Ventura, CA 93002.

Rohde's Inc.—(Organic products, books, and animal supplies) 972-864-1934, 1651 Wall St., Garland, TX 75041.

ORGANIC ROSE PROGRAM

Roses should only be grown organically since they are one of the best medicinal and culinary herbs in the world. When they are loaded with toxic pesticides and other chemicals, that use is gone, or at least it should be. Drinking rose hip tea after spraying the plants with synthetic poisons is a really bad idea. For best results with roses, here's the program:

SELECTION: Choose adapted roses such as antiques, Austins, and well proven hybrids. The old roses will have the largest and most vitamin C filled hips. *Rugosa* roses have the most vitamin C.

PLANTING: Prepare beds by mixing the following into existing soil to form a raised bed: 6" compost, ½–1" lava sand, 20 lbs. of alfalfa meal, 20 lbs. cottonseed meal, 40 lbs. of soft rock phosphate, 20 lbs. of sul-po-mag, 5 lbs. of sulfur, and 20 lbs. of horticultural cornmeal per 1,000 sq. ft. Soak the bare roots or rootball in water with 1 tablespoon of seaweed per gallon and 1 tablespoon of natural apple cider vinegar or commercial bio-stimulant. Settle soil around plants with water—no tamping.

MULCHING: After planting, cover all the soil in the beds with one inch of aged pecan shells followed by 2–3" of shredded native tree trimmings, shredded hardwood bark, or other coarse-textured mulch. Do not pile the mulch up on the stems of the roses.

WATERING: If possible, save and use rainwater. If not, add 1 tablespoon of natural apple cider vinegar per gallon of water. If all that fails, just use tap water but don't over-water. Avoid salty well water if possible.

Organic Rose Program (continued)

FERTILIZING PROGRAM

Round #1

(February 1–15)—Organic fertilizer at 20 lbs./1,000 sq. ft. (i.e. Garden-Ville, GreenSense, Bradfield, Maestro-Gro, Bioform Dry, Sustane, or natural meals), lava sand at 80 lbs./1,000 sq. ft., and sugar at 5 lbs./1,000 sq. ft. Add horticultural cornmeal at 20 lbs./1,000 sq. ft. For thirps control, apply beneficial nematodes to soil before buds beigin to form.

Round #2

(June 1–15)— Organic fertilizer at 20 lbs./1,000 sq. ft., Texas greensand @ at 80 lbs./1,000 sq. ft., or soft rock phosphate at 30 lbs./1,000 sq. ft. if in acid soil areas.
Add horticultural cornmeal at 20 lbs./1,000 sq. ft.

Round #3

(September15–30)—Organic fertilizer at 20 lbs./1,000 sq. ft., Sul-Po-Mag at 20 lbs./1,000 sq. ft. In sandy acid soils use soft rock phosphate instead at 30 lbs./1,000 sq. ft.

SPRAY PROGRAM:

Spray Garrett Juice every two weeks or at least monthly. First spray as new leaves emerge. For insect infestations, add garlic tea or, for tougher pests, orange oil. For diseases such as black spot and powder mildew, add potassium bicarbonate at 1 rounded tablespoon per gallon of spray.

ORGANIC PECAN AND FRUIT TREE PROGRAM

Pecans can be grown organically and no, you don't have to spray toxic pesticides. Plant adapted varieties. The native varieties are the best choices. Plant the trees in wide, ugly holes, backfill with soil from hole (no amendments), settle the soil with water (no tamping), add a 1" layer of lava sand and compost mix, finish with a 3–5" layer of coarse textured mulch. Do not stake, wrap trunk, or cut back the top. Those who say to dig a small round hole are undereducated. Mechanical aeration of the root zone of existing trees is beneficial, but tilling, disking, or plowing destroys feeder roots and should never be done.

FERTILIZING PROGRAM FOR PECANS AND FRUIT TREES
Round #1

(February 1–15)—Organic fertilizer at 20 lbs./1,000 sq. ft. (i.e. Garden-Ville, GreenSense, Bradfield, Bioform Dry, MaestroGro, Sustane or natural meals. Lava sand at 80 lbs./1,000 sq. ft. and sugar at 5 lbs./1,000 sq. ft.

Round #2

(June 1–15)—Organic fertilizer at 20 lbs./1,000 sq. ft. Texas greensand at 40–80 lbs./1,000 sq. ft., and horticultural cornmeal at 20 lbs./1,000 sq. ft.

Round #3

(September 15–30)—Organic fertilizer at 20 lbs./1,000 sq. ft., and Sul-Po-Mag at 20 lbs./1,000 sq. ft. or soft rock phosphate if in acid soils.

Note: Once soil health has been achieved, the schedule can probably be cut to one application a year.

Large scale pecan orchards can use livestock manure or compost at 1–2 tons/acre per year along with establishing green manure cover crops. Lava sand and other rock powders can be applied any time of the year.

Organic Pecan and Fruit Tree Program (continued)

FRUIT AND NUT SPRAY PROGRAM

Spray Garrett Juice at least monthly. Add garlic tea if pests appear.

SPRAY SCHEDULE

First spraying at pink bud. Use additional sprayings as time and budget allow.

Second spraying after flowers have fallen. For best results spray every two weeks, but at least once a month.

Third spraying about June 15.

Fourth spraying last week in August.

INSECT RELEASE

Trichogramma wasps	Weekly releases of 10,000–20,000 eggs per acre or residential lot starting at bud break for 3 weeks.
Green lacewings weekly	Release at 4,000 eggs per acre or residential lot for one month.
Ladybugs	Release 1,500–2,000 adult beetles per 1,000 sq. ft. at the first sign of shiny honeydew on foliage.

Very little pruning is needed or recommended. Maintain cover crops and/or natural mulch under the trees year round. Never cultivate the soil under pecan and fruit trees.

GLOSSARY

ACID SOIL: Soils with a pH less than 7. If the pH is near 6, a soil is con sidered slightly or moderately acid; if below 5.5, it is very acid.

AERATION: A mechanical process of punching holes or ripping the soil, used to relieve the effects of soil compaction.

AEROBIC: An environment containing oxygen. In the soil, aerobic conditions favor organisms that oxidize organic residues and produce carbon dioxide as a major byproduct.

AGRISPON: A mineral and plant extract product that stimulates microorganisms and basic soil and plant functions. Manufactured in Texas by Appropriate Technologies.

ALKALINE SOIL: Soils with a pH greater than 7.

AMMONIUM NITRATE: 33–0–0 (NH_4-NO_3) A water soluble chemical compound containing approximately 33.5 percent nitrogen, one half of which is the ammonia form and one half in the nitrate form. Should not be used.

AMMONIUM PHOSPHATE: A solid fertilizer material manufactured by reacting ammonia with phosphoric acid. Should not be used.

AMMONIUM SULFATE: 21–0–0 [$(NH_4)_2SO_4$] A solid material manufactured by reacting ammonia with sulfuric acid. Should not be used.

ANAEROBIC: Without oxygen. Anaerobic decomposition is less efficient than aerobic organisms. Nitrogen fixation by free-living organisms usually occurs under anaerobic conditions.

ANHYDROUS AMMONIA: 82–0–0 (NH3) A gas containing approximately 82 percent nitrogen. Under pressure, ammonia gas is changed to a liquid and usually is stored and transported in this form. Anhydrous ammonia is used to make most of the solid forms of nitrogenous fertilizers and also is used for direct application to the soil either as a gas or in the form of aqua ammonia. The most soil-destructive fertilizer in the world.

ANION: An ion with a negative electrical charge. Sulfur, phosphorus, boron, chlorine, and molybdenum exist in the soil as anions.

ANION EXCHANGE: A condition, analogous to cation exchange, where one anion can replace another at the surface of a clay mineral.

ANTIDESICCANTS: Liquid sprays used to coat the foliage of plants for the purpose of reducing transpiration in hot weather and increasing cold tolerance in winter.

BACILLUS THURINGIENSIS (Bt): Biological insecticides that specifically target caterpillars and other problem insects.

BANDING FERTILIZER: The process of spreading fertilizer in bands rather than broadcasting it. The fertilize may be spread along a line about two inches to the side of a planted seed and sometimes two inches below. It is considered one of the best methods for utilizing commercial soluble fertilizers, especially phosphorus.

BAT GUANO: Bat poop.

BIODIVERSITY: Biodiversity of life is not just important, it's critical. The outstanding characteristics of Nature are variety and dynamic stability. A healthy situation exists when we create ranches, farms, gardens, and landscapes that have a complex mix of microorganisms, insects, animals, and plants. To understand Nature is to grasp the concept that Nature is a whole and can't be subdivided. Everything relates to everything else.

BLOOD MEAL: A dry, organic fertilizer made of the blood from slaughterhouses. Normal analysis will be approximately 12–0–0.

BONE MEAL: Cooked bones ground to a meal without any of the gelatin or glue removed. Steamed bone meal has been steamed under pressure to dissolve and remove part of the gelatin.

BORAX: A salt (sodium borate) used in fertilizer as a source of the minor plant-food element boron. Borax contains about 11 percent of the element boron. It is available in food stores and is a suitable fertilizer for supplying boron. Use only in very small amounts.

BORDEAUX MIX: A fungicide and insecticide made by mixing solutions of copper sulfate and lime, or of copper arsenate and phenols. Use the first one.

BUFFER CAPACITY: The degree to which a substance can resist changes in its characteristics.

BURNED LIME: Limestone heated to drive out carbon dioxide. Same as quicklime.

CALCAREOUS: Containing a high percentage of calcium or calcium carbonate.

CALCITE: Limestone containing mostly calcium carbonate, $CaCO_3$. A more common name is ground agricultural limestone.

CALCIUM CARBONATE: The principal component of calcitic limestone and one of the principal components of dolomitic limestone, of which magnesium carbonate, $MgCO_3$ is the other. Marl and oyster shells also are composed primarily of calcium carbonate.

CARBOHYDRATES: Stabilized structures of sugars. Carbohydrates form the skeleton of the plant, and they are a means for storing energy for a long period of time.

CATION EXCHANGE: A process in which the small number of cations dissolved in the soil water (soluble cations) change place with the much larger number of cations associated with the soil micelles (exchangeable cations).

CATION EXCHANGE CAPACITY: A measure of the ability of the soil components to attract cations and hold them in exchangeable form. The exchange capacity depends upon the amount of clay, the type of clay, the organic content, and the degree of humification of the organic matter.

CEC: An abbreviation for cation exchange capacity.

CHELATION: The chemical process by which an organic substance binds a cation having more than one electrical charge. Chelation is similar to cation exchange. Cation exchange holds the majority of the major cation nutrients (calcium, magnesium, potassium), while chelation holds the cation trace elements (copper, iron, magnanese, zinc).

CLIPPINGS: Leaves cut off by mowing.

C/N RATIO: An abbreviation for carbon/nitrogen ratio.

COLLOIDAL: A state of matter where finely divided particles of one substance are suspended in another.

COLLOIDAL PHOSPHATE: Waste material from rock-phosphate mining operation. An excellent, slow-release source of phosphorus, calcium, and trace elements.

COMPACTION: The pressing together of soil particles by foot or vehicular traffic.

COMPANION PLANTING: Using different plants together that assist one another with insect and disease control.

COMPOST: Nature's fertilizer created by the rotting of vegetable and animal matter.

COMPOSTED MANURE: Animal manure that has been taken through the process of natural composting in order to kill pathogens and weed seed.

COOL-SEASON TURFGRASS: Those turfgrasses primarily used in the northern United States, such as Kentucky bluegrass, tall fescue, and ryegrass.

COPPERAS: Ferrous (iron) sulfate used as a trace nutrient fertilizer, especially in alkaline soils.

COPPER SULFATE: ($CuSO_4 \cdot 5H_2O$) Most common source of copper for fertilizer. Also used as an insecticide and fungicide. A common name is blue vitriol.

COTTONSEED MEAL: Fertilizer meal made from ground cottonseed.

COVER CROP: A crop that improves the soil on which it is grown. Many plants are sown primarily as cover crops to cover the ground, improve it, and protect it for a succeeding cash crop. Other plants, such as alfalfa, clover, and most grass-legume sods, can serve as both a cash crop and a cover crop.

CROSS-POLLINATE: To apply pollen of a male flower to the stigma or female part of another flower.

CURCULIO, PLUM: Worm that attacks the fruit of plums and other orchard trees.

CUTTING HEIGHT: The distance between the ground and the blades of the mower.

CYTOKININ: A plant hormone that can modify plant development by stimulating or altering the cellular RNA.

DAMPING OFF: A disease of seeds and young seedlings caused by fungi.

DENITRIFICATION: The conversion of nitrates in the soil to some form of gaseous nitrogen, which escapes into the atmosphere and is lost.

DIACIDE: Organic insecticide made primarily from diatomaceous earth and natural pyrethrum.

DIAMMONIUM PHOSPHATE: (21–53–0) A solid fertilizer material made by reacting ammonia with phosphoric acid.

DICOTYLEDON (DICOT): A plant with two seed leaves.

DIOECIOUS: Plants that have the male reproductive system on one plant and the female on another.

DNA: (Deoxyribonucleic acid)
Nucleic acid found in all living cells.

DOLOMITE: A material used for liming soils in areas where magnesium as well as calcium are needed. Made by grinding dolomitic limestone, which contains both magnesium carbonate, $MgCO_3$, and calcium carbonate, $CaCO_3$.

DORMANT OIL: Petroleum-based oil used for smothering overwinter insects such as scale.

DORMANT TURF: A brown-colored turf that has temporarily ceased growth due to unfavorable environmental conditions.

EARTHWORM CASTINGS:
Earth worm poop.

EPIPHYTIC: Referring to plants growing without soil and receiving their nutrients from the air.

EPSOM SALTS: Magnesium sulfate. It is used as a fast-acting source of magnesium and sulfur. Normally used as a foliar feed.

EXCHANGEABLE CATIONS:
Those cations that are electrostatically attracted to soil particles. The sum of the exchangeable cations and the soluble cations is considered to constitute the available cations for plant take-up.

FERTIGATION: The application of fertilizer through an irrigation system.

FERTILIZER: Any material or mixture used to supply one or more soil or plant nutrients.

FISH EMULSION: An oily liquid fertilizer made from fish waste or whole fish.

FLOWERS OF SULFUR: Finely granulated sulfur dust, used to acidify an alkaline soil.

FOLIAR BURN: An injury to the leaves of the plant, caused by the application of a fertilizer or pesticide.

FOLIAR SPRAY: Liquid plant nutrients applied by spraying on the foliage.

FOOTPRINTING: Discolored areas, or impressions, left in the lawn from foot traffic when the turf is in the first stage of wilt.

FRENCH DRAIN: A drainage device in which a hole or trench is back-filled with sand or gravel.

FUNGICIDE: A product used to control diseases caused by fungi.

GEOTROPISM: The effect of gravity on plants.

GRANITE SAND: Sand made from weathered or ground up granite rock.

GREEN MANURE: A cover crop used to smother weeds, to protect the soil, and to hold nutrients that might otherwise be leached. Traditionally a green manure is planted after the harvest of a cash crop, but an alternative is a "living mulch," where a cover crop is sown before harvesting the cash crop.

GREENSAND: A material called glauconite, which is a naturally deposited undersea, iron potassium silicate. It's an excellent source of potash with a normal analysis of 0–1–5. It's best used with other fertilizers.

GUANO: Decomposed dried excrement of birds and bats used for fertilizer purposes. The most commonly known guano comes from islands off the coast of Peru and is derived from the excrement of sea fowl. It is high in nitrogen and phosphate, and at one time was a major fertilizer in this country.

GYPSUM: The common name for calcium sulfate, a mineral used in the fertilizer industy as a source of calcium and sulfur. It is a good source of sulfur and is also used to improve alkaline soils having a high sodium content.

HAY: Grass, clover, or the like that is cut while still green and used as a fodder or mulch.

HERBICIDE: A product used for weed control.

HUMUS: The Latin word for soil or earth. It is the broken-down form of organic matter.

HYDROGEN PEROXIDE: An oxygenating compound used for soil conditioning and bacteria fighting.

HYDROMULCHING: A method of seeding using a mixture of seed, fertilizer, and mulch, sprayed in a solution on the soil surface.

HYDROSEEDING: Same as hydromulching but without the mulch.

HYDROSPRIGGING: Same as hydromulching but uses sprigs instead of seed.

ION: An electrostatically charged atom formed when a salt is dissolved in water. The dissolved salt breaks up into both positively and negatively charged ions.
IONIC CHARGE: The electrical charge associated with ions. Cations have a positive electrical charge and anions a negative charge.

INSECTICIDE: A product used to control insects.

INTEGRATED PEST MANAGEMENT: Buzzword for using a little bit of organics and a varying bit of chemicals.

IRRIGATION, AUTOMATIC: An irrigation system using preset timing devices.

LANGBEINITE: Sul-Po-Mag.

LAYERING, SOIL: An undesirable stratification of a soil.

LEACHING: The movement (usually loss) of dissolved nutrients as water percolates through the soil.

LEATHER TANKAGE: Waste from the leather tanning industry.

LIME: Technically, lime is calcium oxide. In agricultural usage, however, the term is used to denote any liming material.

LIME SULFUR: Organic pesticide used for disease control.

LOCALIZED DRY SPOT: An area of soil that resists wetting.

MAGNESIA: Magnesium oxide, used as an emergency source of magnesium.

MAGNESIUM SULFATE: A soluble salt used as a source of magnesium. Common forms are the mineral kieserite and epsom salts.

MANALFA: Organic fertilizer made from a blend of livestock manure and alfalfa.

MANGANESE SULFATE: A solid chemical compound used as a source of manganese for plants.

MANURE: Manure most commonly refers to animal dung, but the term is also used in association with green manuring.

MILORGANITE: Sewer sludge fertilizer from Milwaukee. Hou-Actinite is a better product for those in the South.

MINERAL OIL: Oil made from refined petroleum products.

MOLYBDENUM: One of the essential micronutrients.

MONOECIOUS: Plants that have male and female flowers on the same plant.

MYCORRHIZAE: Fungi which penetrate roots of plants to extract carbohydrates. Its unique value is that in return it passes mineral nutrients to the plant. It can be a major source of available phosphorus. It is similar to the rhizobia bacteria that inhabit legume roots and fix nitrogen.

NECTAR: A sweet liquid secreted by plants. The main raw material of honey.

NEMATODES: Small hair-like organisms that attack root systems and other soilborne organisms.

NITRATE INHIBITORS: Substances that retard the ability of soil organisms to transform ammonium to nitrates. Their purpose is to avoid the denitrification which occurs with heavy fertilizer applications of urea, ammonium salts, or liquid ammonia.

NITRATE OF SODA: Sodium nitrate ($NaNO_3$) A fertilizer material containing approximately 16 percent nitrogen. The principal source of sodium nitrate has been the natural deposits of the salt in Chile. It is also produced synthetically. Do not use.

NITRIFICATION: A process which takes place in the soil whereby soil microorganisms form nitrates from organic matter and the ammonia forms of nitrogen.

NPK: A shorthand notation for "Nitrogen-Phosphate-Potash."

OPEN POLLINATED: Unlike hybrids, plants that will return true from seed.

ORGANIC MATTER: Organic substances in differing stages of decay, varying from litter to very stable humus.

OVERSEEDING: Seeding a dormant turf with a cool-season grass in order to provide color during the winter.

PEAT: A low-quality humus in which the nitrogen is completely lost through anaerobic fermentation.

PESTICIDE: A chemical used to control any turfgrass pest, such as weeds, insects, and diseases.

pH: An abbreviation for potential hydrogen, used chemically to express the hydrogen ion concentration of a solution. More simply, pH is a scale from 1 to 14, used to denote the relative intensity of acidity or alkalinity. A neutral solution, or soil, has a pH of 7.0. Values below 7.0 denote more acid conditions, and those above 7.0 more alkaline conditions.

PHOSPHATE: The fertilizer oxide form of phosphorus (P_2O_5).

PHOSPHORIC ACID: 0–52–0 to 0–55–0 (H_3PO_4) An inorganic acid used in the manufacture of concentrated calcium phosphates and ammonium phosphates and sometimes for direct application through irrigation water.

PHYTOPHTHORA: Latin name for a genus of fungi that causes plant disease, generally a root and crown-rot pathogen.

PHOTOSYNTHESIS: Nature's process of manufacturing carbohydrates from carbon dioxide (CO_2) and water (H_2O) with the use of light energy and green plant pigment called chlorophyll.

PLANT METABOLISM: Those functions of a plant that use energy stored in sugars and carbohydrates to enable the plant to grow and reproduce.

PLUGGING: Establishing a turfgrass using plugs of sod.

POLLEN: A mass of microspores in a seed plant. Looks like a fine dust.

POLYSACCHARIDES: Carbohydrates (complex sugars) of high molecular weight including starch and cellulose.

POTASH: A term used to denote potassium oxide (K_2O) equivalent of materials containing potassium.

POTASSIUM CHLORIDE: 0–60–0 (KCl) Muriate of potash.

POTASSIUM MAGNESIUM SULFATE: ($2MgSO_4$ K_2SO_4) Also called Sul-Po-Mag and langbeinite. From natural salt deposits primarily in New Mexico and some European countries. Organic source of K, Mg, and S.

POTASSIUM SULFATE: (K_2SO_4) A solid material with a K_2O equivalent of 45 to 52 percent. Also called sulfate of potash.

PROTEINS: The active, amino acid components of a growing plant. Proteins carry out the bodily activities of the plant, using the energy from sugars and carbohydrates.

PYRETHRUM: Natural insecticide made from the powder of the crushed painted daisy, *Chrysanthemum cin-erariaefolium.* Very toxic.

QUICKLIME: Burned lime, roasted to drive out carbon dioxide and increase the solubility.

REEL MOWER: A mower that cuts grass by means of a reel guiding the leaves against the cutting edge of the bedknife.

RENOVATION: Improving the vigor of a low-quality soil.

RHIZOBIA: A group of bacteria that penetrates the roots of legumes, extracting carbohydrates from the plant, and capable of fixing atmospheric nitrogen.

RHIZOME: A below-ground stem capable of producing a new plant.

RHIZOSPHERE: The soil area immediately adjacent to the root hairs of plants.

ROCK POWDERS: Naturally occurring materials with fertilizing value. The most common rock powders are limestone, rock phosphate, granite dust, greensand, langbeinite (sulfate of potash magnesia), and basalt.

ROOT NODULES: Nodules attached to the roots of legumes and certain nonlegumes. These nodules contain nitrogen fixing bacteria or nematodes.

ROTARY MOWER: A mower that cuts grass with a high-speed blade that runs parallel to the soil surface.

SALT INDEX: The relation of solubilities of chemical compounds. Most nitrogen and potash compounds have a high index, and phosphate compounds have a low index. When applied too close to seed or on foliage, the ones with high indexes can cause plants to wilt or die.

SCALD: Grass that dies under "standing water."

SCALPING: The excessive removal of leaves during mowing, leaving mostly stems.

SEAWEED: Saltwater plants used for fertilizer.

SECONDARY ELEMENTS: The secondary plant food elements as traditionally defined are calcium, magnesium, and sulfur.

SLAG: A byproduct of steel, containing lime, phosphate, and small amounts of other plant food elements such as sulfur, manganese, and iron.

SOAP: A cleansing and emulsifying agent made by action of alkali on fat or fatty acids.

SOD: Plugs, squares, or strips of turf still connected to soil.

SOFT ROCK PHOSPHATE: Colloidal rock phosphate. A by-product of rock phosphate mining.

SOIL: An ecological system consisting of inorganic minerals, organic matter, and living organisms.

SOIL pH: The pH of the water in soil. It controls the availability of phosphorus and trace elements and the diversity of soil organisms. The soil pH for most soils is in the range 5.0 to 9.0, with 7.0 being neutral.

SOIL STRUCTURE: The distribution and size of aggregates in the soil. A good soil structure contains aggregates of widely varying size.

SPRIGGING: Establishing a lawn using sprigs or stolons.

STOLON: An above-ground stem capable of growing a new plant.

STRAW: The above-ground vegetative growth of a plant, usually a small grain or annual legume.

SUGAR: The direct product of photosynthesis. Sugars store the energy absorbed from the sun in the plant leaves.

SULFATE OF POTASH-MAGNESIA: ($2MgSO_4$ K_2SO_4) A naturally occurring solid material, also called langbeinite, found in salt deposits primarily in New Mexico and in several European countries. The commercial product usually has a K_2O equivalent of about 21 percent, and contains 53 percent magnesium sulfate and not more than 2½ percent chlorine. It is used in fertilizer as a source of both potash and magnesium.

SULFUR: Normally referred to as a secondary element. It is actually a primary nutrient and is critical in the synthesis of proteins.

SUL-PO-MAG: Mined material consisting of sulfur, potassium, and magnesium. (See sulfate of potash- magnesia.)

SUPERPHOSPHATE: The first manufactured phosphorus fertilizer, prepared originally by dissolving bones in sulfuric acid. 0–18–0 to 0–20–0.

SUPERPHOSPHORIC ACID: 0– 67–0 to 0–76–0.

TANKAGE: Process tankage is made from leather scrap, wool, and other inert nitrogenous materials by steaming under pressure with or without addition of acid. This treatment increases the availability of the nitrogen to plants.

THATCH: A layer of organic matter that develops between the soil and the base of the plant.

TOPDRESSING: Spreading a thin layer of soil on the lawn to smooth the surface.

TRANSITION ZONE: An east– west zone through the middle of the U.S. between the northern area, growing cold-season turfgrasses, and the southern area, growing warm-season turfgrasses.

TRIPLE SUPERPHOSPHATE:
Rock- phosphate dissolved in phosphoric acid.

UREA: 45–0–0 - $CO(NH_2)_2$ A solid synthetic organic material containing approximately 45 percent nitrogen.

UREA-FORM: Synthetic fertilizer (38–0–0).

VERTICAL MOWING: The use of mechanical device that has vertically rotating blades for thatch control.

VOLATILIZATION: The process of liquid becoming a gas.

WARM-SEASON TURFGRASS:
Those turfgrasses used primarily in the southern United States, such as Bermuda grass, St. Augustine grass, zoysia grass, centipedegrass, and buffalo grass.

WILT: The discoloration and folding of leaves caused by either excessively dry or excessively wet conditions.

ZINC SULFATE: ($ZnSO_4 \cdot 7H_2O$)
White vitriol, a solid material used as a source of zinc.

INDEX